IMAGES
of Rail

WESTERN &
ATLANTIC RAILROAD

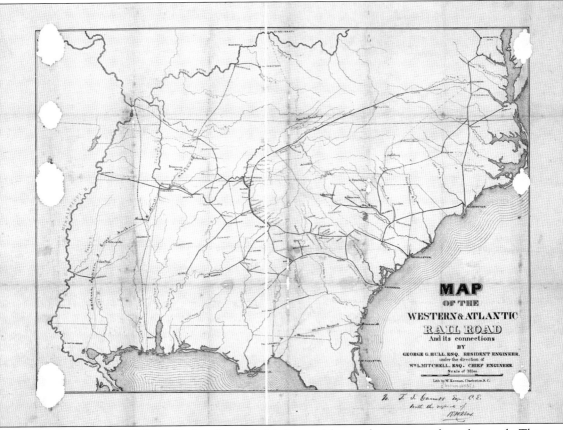

The Western & Atlantic Railroad provided Atlanta with a vital connection from the north. This map, published between 1850 and 1855, shows the railroad's integral role in the Southeastern railroad network and its crucial links with railroads in Atlanta; Chattanooga, Tennessee; Rome, Georgia; and Dalton, Georgia. (Courtesy of the University of North Carolina at Chapel Hill.)

On the Cover: On April 13, 1887, the Western & Atlantic offered an excursion from Chattanooga to Atlanta for the families of members of the International Association of Car Accountants. The famous *General* locomotive pulled the train, and when it reached Allatoona Pass, the group disembarked for a photograph in front of the train. (Courtesy of Georgia Archives, Vanishing Georgia Collection, brt138-91.)

IMAGES
of Rail

WESTERN &
ATLANTIC RAILROAD

Todd DeFeo

ARCADIA
PUBLISHING

Published by Arcadia Publishing
Charleston, South Carolina

Printed in the United States of America

Library of Congress Control Number: 2018967898

For all general information, please contact Arcadia Publishing:
Telephone 843-853-2070
Fax 843-853-0044
E-mail sales@arcadiapublishing.com
For customer service and orders:
Toll-Free 1-888-313-2665

Visit us on the Internet at www.arcadiapublishing.com

*This book is dedicated to my lovely wife, Ruth, and to our
son Thomas. You'll be with me "Everywhere I Go."*

CONTENTS

ACKNOWLEDGMENTS

From my office, I can hear the whistle of trains operating along the Western & Atlantic Railroad. It is a far cry from the small steam locomotives that ran along the line starting roughly 170 years ago. These are modern diesel-electric engines pulling massive trains packed with a range of goods and commodities. Just as it was back then, the Western & Atlantic is an integral part of so many North Georgia communities.

Writing this book would not have been possible if not for the many museums and research centers dedicated to preserving railroad history for future generations. They are the real heroes. They keep the memory of yesterday's railroads alive for today's students of history and those to come tomorrow.

These museums include the Southern Museum of Civil War & Locomotive History in Kennesaw, Georgia; the Southeastern Railway Museum in Duluth, Georgia; the Adairsville Depot History Museum in Adairsville, Georgia; the Bartow History Museum in Cartersville, Georgia; the Tunnel Hill Heritage Center and Museum in Tunnel Hill, Georgia; the Marietta History Museum in Marietta, Georgia; and the Chattanooga Public Library in Chattanooga, Tennessee.

I am particularly appreciative of the many museums and archivists who provided me with invaluable research assistance. I am even more grateful for my wife, Ruth, for helping me develop this book, and to my parents for helping me proofread drafts and making sure it was at least somewhat coherent.

A book of this nature is not a comprehensive account of everyone associated with the railroad. Nor is it a retelling of every episode, train wreck, and corporate event associated with the line. It is but a brief overview of the Western & Atlantic and its role shaping a region.

INTRODUCTION

It is hard to imagine Georgia without Atlanta. But, at the dawn of the 19th century, the city did not exist. The state's capital was located in the tiny hamlet of Louisville, where it remained until 1806, and its power centers included Augusta and Savannah.

That began to change in the fall of 1837 when Col. Stephen Harriman Long—or perhaps one of his colleagues—drove a stake into the ground at a point located roughly seven miles east of the Chattahoochee River. The rather unceremonious happening had far-reaching effects still felt today.

Long, the chief engineer of the state-owned Western & Atlantic Railroad, and his team had identified the area that would become the city of Atlanta, today the economic engine of the Southeast. Ironically, Long thought the area would be nothing more than a railroad crossroad, and he opted to set up shop in the city of Marietta, Georgia. "The Terminus will be a good location for one tavern, a blacksmith shop, a grocery store, and nothing else," Long said.

While he might have misjudged how important this terminus would grow to become, he did not underestimate the importance of the Western & Atlantic Railroad. Long surveyed the route starting on May 12, 1837, and finished in November 1840. Construction on the railroad began in March 1838, proceeding slowly at first. It took 12 years to complete.

At its southern end, the community that grew up around the railroad was initially named Terminus. It was renamed Marthasville in 1843 and Atlanta in 1847. The original city's limits extended a mile and a half in every direction from the railroad depot built on the site.

In December 1841, the state suspended work on the railroad north of the Etowah River, but the decision was a relatively temporary one. In 1842, the railroad's original terminus moved a short distance to an area that is today beneath the Central Avenue viaduct at Underground Atlanta. A few years later, in 1850, the zero-mile post, a marble mile marker, was driven into the ground at this point. While Long left his position as the railroad's chief engineer in November 1840, the wheels were in motion, and the community that started with a stake in the ground grew to more than 9,500 residents in about 20 years.

The Western & Atlantic was not the first railroad in the state. In 1831, the Georgia Railroad organized to build eastward from Augusta. Two years later, the Central Railroad and Canal Company chartered to build between Savannah and Macon, and the Monroe Railroad Company, later reorganized as the Macon and Western Railroad, was to build from Macon to Forsyth. The Western & Atlantic would be the conduit that connected these railroads with important western points, including the Tennessee River.

The story of the Western & Atlantic Railroad is a combination of vision, gumption, and engineering fortitude. The workers who built the road between Atlanta and Chattanooga etched a line in the earth that largely remains unmoved to this day. They carved through mountains and crossed rivers and wound a path through North Georgia's hilly countryside until they built the "crookedest road under the sun," as Supt. John W. Lewis called it in the 1860 report.

"When it is understood that at the time this work was begun there were only a few railroads in the United States; that the science of railroad engineering was in its infancy; and that the country traversed by the Western and Atlantic Railroad is crossed by many streams and high ridges, Colonel Long's location stands out as a remarkable achievement," historian James Houstoun Johnston wrote in a 1930s history of the railroad.

The Western & Atlantic's impact on the state of Georgia and the cities and towns between Atlanta and Chattanooga cannot be overstated. The railroad created a lifeline for communities and was vitally important to the South's war effort. It also helped the Union defeat the Confederacy in the Civil War.

Perhaps, many people associate the railroad with the Great Locomotive Chase of 1862, when Union spies stole a locomotive with the intent of destroying this important rail line. While the plan failed, the line later played an important role when Gen. William T. Sherman marched southward to Atlanta. The railroad "'should be the pride of every true American' because 'by reason of its existence the Union was saved,' " Sherman is often quoted as saying. He excelled at using railroads as part of his supply chain during his march to Atlanta.

After the war, the State Road, as the line was often called, continued its role in shaping North Georgia communities. One tangible way was by transporting throngs of tourists looking to retrace the steps of soldiers who fought in some of the Civil War's most famous battles. When the Western & Atlantic name faded from the region's collective lexicon, the line reinvented itself under new banners: first as part of the Nashville, Chattanooga & St. Louis Railway, then the Louisville & Nashville Railroad and others before CSX Transportation.

Even today, the line is a backbone for local industries. As Atlanta grapples with its transportation future, it is worth noting that without the Western & Atlantic Railroad, Atlanta would not be the city it is today. "The Western and Atlantic Railroad is a final success; which should be to every citizen of the State, to which it belongs, a matter of not only laudable State pride, but of gratitude," Superintendent Lewis wrote in the 1859 annual report.

While the State of Georgia still owns the railroad, private companies have leased the line since 1870. Even with many upgrades over the years, the route still largely follows the one Colonel Long identified more than 180 years ago.

One

CALM BEFORE THE STORM

The impetus for developing a network of railroads in Georgia has South Carolina to thank. The South Carolina Canal and Railroad Company was chartered in 1827 to build a railroad from Charleston to Hamburg, South Carolina, a city situated on the Savannah River across from Augusta, Georgia.

After the invention of the cotton gin in 1793, cotton production across the region exploded. Residents in Georgia and South Carolina, traditional strongholds of cotton production, needed both cheaper transportation and manufactured goods, requiring improvements to the region's transportation infrastructure.

In 1825, the State of Georgia created a Board of Public Works to explore transportation improvements within the state. A survey for a railroad was conducted the following year. The state appointed Hamilton Fulton as chief engineer, and future state governor Wilson Lumpkin helped Fulton survey the route.

"After laborious and instrumental examination of the country, from Milledgeville to Chattanooga, it was the opinion of Mr. Fulton and myself that a rail road could be located to advantage between the two points above named, but that a canal was impracticable," Lumpkin later wrote. "It is a very remarkable fact too, that the route selected by Mr. Fulton and myself, a large portion of it then in an Indian Country, and but little known to civilized men, should in its whole distance have varied so slightly from the location of our present rail roads now in operation."

"Attempts to meet these needs by river improvements, canals and turnpikes, were made in various quarters, but with little success," historian Ulrich Bonnell Phillips wrote in a 1906 history of the railroad. "Some resource of much greater efficiency was required. The building of the Western and Atlantic Railroad was the decisive step in solving the problem."

Construction proceeded slowly at first, and larger economic conditions, such as the Panic of 1837, did little to help construction. But, by 1842, tracks were in place between Atlanta and Marietta. The railroad was still far from complete, and locals liked to say "the railroad didn't start nowhere or go nowhere."

They were not wrong, but on Christmas Eve of that year, a locomotive and a single car pulled out of Atlanta, marking a new era in the city's history. The locomotive on that historic journey was the *Florida*, in use on the Georgia Rail Road since 1837. When the Western & Atlantic needed motive power for their line, it purchased the steamer. The problem was there was no way to relocate the locomotive to Atlanta by rail. So, the Georgia Rail Road steamed the engine to its then terminus in Madison, Georgia. There, workers loaded it on a cart, and a team of 16 mules hauled it to Atlanta, where it could enter service on the Western & Atlantic.

For the historic first journey along the Western & Atlantic, the engine pulled a single car—either a boxcar or a passenger car built at the penitentiary. Most accounts name the engineer as William F. Adair, while other sources indicate Jim Rustin was at the throttle. When the train reached the bridge over the Chattahoochee River, it stopped. Passengers disembarked because they feared the bridge would not support the train. They walked across the trestle; the bridge held, and the locomotive glided across "like a being of the clouds," a letter writer to a local newspaper recalled in February 1843. The Western & Atlantic was, at least in a small way, a functioning railroad, though it would be another three years before some semblance of regular operations began.

"The place appears to be well selected for the connecting of other roads with it," the letter writer also noted. "There is some magnificent scenery along this State Road, natural as well as artificial. To see a steam car walking like 'a thing of life,' through these mountains, and over rivers and creeks and ravines, is grand to look upon."

By January 1845, because of the state's finances, Georgia governor George W. Crawford offered the road for sale, but it did not sell.

By 1849, the railroad had 10 locomotives on its roster, including the *Yonah*, which the railroad purchased in April 1849. The steamer was listed in "good order" and would later enter the annals of history for its role in the Great Locomotive Chase of 1862. Only one locomotive, the *Alabama*, which the railroad bought in September 1845, was listed as operating west of the not-yet-built tunnel through Chetoogeta Mountain.

Although completing tracks between Atlanta and Marietta was a feat worth celebrating, it represented only a small portion of the line. One of the biggest hurdles facing workers was Chetoogeta Mountain in North Georgia, which required digging a 1,477-foot-long tunnel through limestone, chert, clay, gravel, and mud. The community that grew up around the tunnel was later named Tunnel Hill.

At 11:00 a.m. on October 31, 1849, workers completed the headings for the tunnel through Chetoogeta Mountain. "It was a day long and anxiously looked for by the officers of the road, the contractors and workmen," the *Federal Union* reported. "When the light first pierced through the aperture, we understand it was a moment of great rejoicing and that some rich scenes were enacted under the mountain." In a letter published in the November 1, 1849, edition of the newspaper, William L. Mitchell said, "The excitement was so great that nothing could control it, all work was suspended, and the feeling to celebrate this peaceful victory over nature's obstacles in some benefiting manner was universal."

The tunnel formally opened for traffic on May 9, 1850. "The stupendous monument of enterprise and skill in civil engineering . . . is at length completed," the *Southern Recorder* newspaper of May 14, 1850, reported.

On the eve of the Civil War, the railroad had more than 45 locomotives on its active roster, including the *R.C. Jackson*, a freight "engine of medium size" that the Western & Atlantic built itself and placed in service in September 1860, plus four more engines that were "worn out and condemned." "But, in absence of any legislative action, I shall not feel authorized to sell them," Supt. John W. Lewis said in a September 30, 1860, report to Gov. Joseph E. Brown. He noted, "The Road at no time of your administration, nor at any other time, has been in so perfect condition as at the present time."

Wilson Lumpkin, Georgia's governor from 1831 to 1835, is often regarded as the "Father of the Western & Atlantic." Lumpkin strongly advocated for improved transportation within the state and participated in the state's first railroad survey in 1826. When the name Terminus was changed to Marthasville, it was in honor of Lumpkin's daughter Martha. (Courtesy of the Library of Congress.)

Wilson Lumpkin

GOVERNOR OF GEORGIA.

TABLE 4.

Locomotives.

Names of Engines.	No. of miles run by each Engine from Sept. 30th, 1847, to Sept 30 1848	Condition of Engines, Sept. 30th, 1848.	How Employed.	Cost of repairs to each Engine from Sept 30, 1847 to Sept. 30th, 1848.	Remarks.
Florida,	8,800	Laid up.	For Passengers.	752 44	Purchased December, 1842.
Alabama,	21,000	On Road in good order.	" "	1,339 69	" Sept. 1845.
Chattanooga,	10,000	" " " "	" Freights.	990 39	" January, 1847.
Tuscaloosa,	23,400	In Shop for Repairs.	" "	569 89	" March, "
Connasauga,	18,080	On Road in good order.	" "	1,057 75	" February, "
Monterey,	18,200	" " " "	" Passengers.	920 06	" November, "
Chickamauga,	2,400	" " " "	" Freights.	143 48	" May, 1848.
Talulah.	568	Laid up for Reprs.	" Passengers.	424 05	" " "
				6,188 75	

Chief engineer William L. Mitchell's 1848 report listed the railroad's eight locomotives and their conditions. The railroad's first locomotive, the *Florida*, ran 8,800 miles between September 30, 1847, and September 30, 1848, but was "laid up" at the time of the report. It operated until about 1858 and was listed as "condemned" in the railroad's 1859 report. (Courtesy of the Digital Library of Georgia.)

Atlanta was a city of approximately 2,500 residents in 1850 but grew to a population of roughly 9,500 by the eve of the Civil War. This postcard, published around 1910, depicts the city during this era and shows Atlanta's first train station, which the Georgia Rail Road and Western & Atlantic Railroad used. A larger car shed opened in 1853. (Courtesy of the Archives Center, National Museum of American History, Smithsonian Institution.)

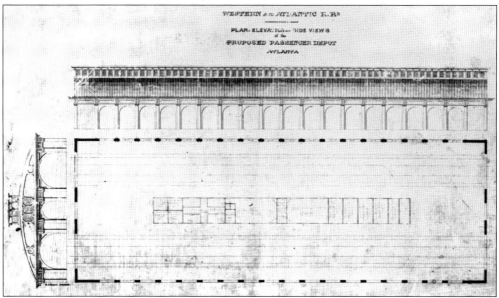

As the Western & Atlantic grew, it needed larger facilities in Atlanta. "I found the Depot Buildings at both ends of the Road, and many of the Ware-Houses at Way-Stations, entirely inadequate for our business," general superintendent William M. Wadley wrote in a September 30, 1852, report. Soon thereafter, the Western & Atlantic Railroad hired Edward A. Vincent to design a modern railroad terminal in Atlanta. (Courtesy of the Southeastern Railway Museum.)

The Western & Atlantic's four-track car shed opened in 1853 and also served the Atlanta & West Point, Georgia and Macon & Western railroads. The depot, colloquially known as the car shed, stood in State Square, the central square of Atlanta in the days before the Civil War. (Both, courtesy of the Library of Congress, Prints & Photographs Division, Civil War Photographs.)

The city of Chattanooga, originally known as Ross' Landing, was incorporated in 1839 along the Tennessee River, an important waterway running from Knoxville, Tennessee, to Paducah, Kentucky. Said one observer in 1847, "If Georgia fails to finish the road or make the appropriation for its completion all is flat in Chattanooga, but the general belief is that she will do it. And then we expect a rush to this place." (Courtesy of the Chattanooga Public Library.)

In Chattanooga, the Western & Atlantic initially used a combination freight and passenger station, built around 1851 at the corner of Market and Ninth Streets. Passenger and freight services were located on the first floor, with offices upstairs. However, much as it did in Atlanta, the railroad soon outgrew its facility and looked to expand. (Courtesy of the Chattanooga Public Library.)

The Western & Atlantic built a new depot with a four-track car shed in Chattanooga in 1858. Eugene LeHardy, chief engineer of the railroad, and John Lother, a master builder, oversaw construction of the shed. Slaves may have made the bricks used in the building's construction. (Courtesy of the Chattanooga Public Library.)

The Western & Atlantic shared the train shed with the Nashville & Chattanooga and the Memphis & Charleston railroads, which began serving Chattanooga during the 1850s. The three railroads helped Chattanooga develop into a vital railroad hub that remains today. During the Civil War, both Confederate and Union troops used this building as a hospital. (Courtesy of the Chattanooga Public Library.)

Building the Western & Atlantic was an extensive construction project at both ends of the line and at points in between. The railroad constructed depots and buildings in nearly every community it bisected, including these structures in Atlanta, photographed by George N. Barnard in 1864. (Courtesy of the National Archives.)

"All these improvements are of a permanent and substantial character—such, I flatter myself, as will prove to be, not only useful ornaments to the Road, but monuments to the Enterprise and Liberality of the People of Georgia," Western & Atlantic general superintendent William Wadley wrote in the railroad's 1852 annual report. This photograph dates from 1864. (Courtesy of the Library of Congress, Prints & Photographs Division, Civil War Photographs.)

Famed Civil War photographer George N. Barnard took this photograph of the Atlanta car shed in 1864, shortly before its destruction. The value of the railroad to the state of Georgia, the Confederacy, and, ultimately, the Union was demonstrated during the Civil War. (Courtesy of the Library of Congress, Prints & Photographs Division, Civil War Photographs.)

To traverse the hilly North Georgia landscape, builders of the Western & Atlantic erected a number of bridges and culverts, including this one over Noonday Creek in Cobb County. The culvert, built around 1848, apparently replaced an earlier bridge. This culvert, seen here during the latter half of the 20th century, was built from cut and dressed fieldstone and includes a stone arch. (Courtesy of the Library of Congress.)

In a September 30, 1860, report to Georgia governor Joseph E. Brown, Western & Atlantic superintendent John W. Lewis referred to the line as "the crookedest road under the sun." This picture, which George Barnard took during the Civil War looking south from atop Allatoona Pass, clearly illustrates how the Western & Atlantic's route traversed the North Georgia landscape. (Courtesy of the Library of Congress, Prints & Photographs Division, Civil War Photographs.)

Building the railroad required several remarkable engineering feats, including the roughly 360-foot-long, 175-foot-deep Allatoona Pass south of Cartersville, which Civil War photographer George Barnard captured here around 1865. Workers carved the pass by hand during the 1840s. Trains ran through the pass for about a century until the line was rerouted during the 1940s. (Courtesy of the J. Paul Getty Museum, Los Angeles.)

The "loss by fire, of the Etowah Bridge, in the midst of the busiest season, undoubtedly deterred both freight and passengers, while it increased the cost of transportation even beyond the extra rate which was assessed to save the Road from loss," Western & Atlantic superintendent James F. Cooper wrote in the railroad's 1855 report. (Photograph by Mathew Brady, courtesy of the National Archives.)

On October 31, 1849, workers completed the headings for a tunnel through Chetoogeta Mountain. In the November 1, 1849, edition of the *Federal Union* newspaper, chief engineer William L. Mitchell wrote, "The excitement was so great that nothing could control it, all work was suspended, and the feeling to celebrate this peaceful victory over nature's obstacles in some benefiting manner was universal." (Photograph by Mathew Brady, courtesy of the National Archives.)

As part of the 1849 celebration of the completion of the headings through Chetoogeta Mountain, industrialist Mark A. Cooper supplied a cannon from his ironworks in Etowah, Georgia. "The roar of Georgia's native cannon over that mountain top indicates that in time of peace we are prepared for war," he ominously said during his remarks. (Courtesy of HathiTrust.)

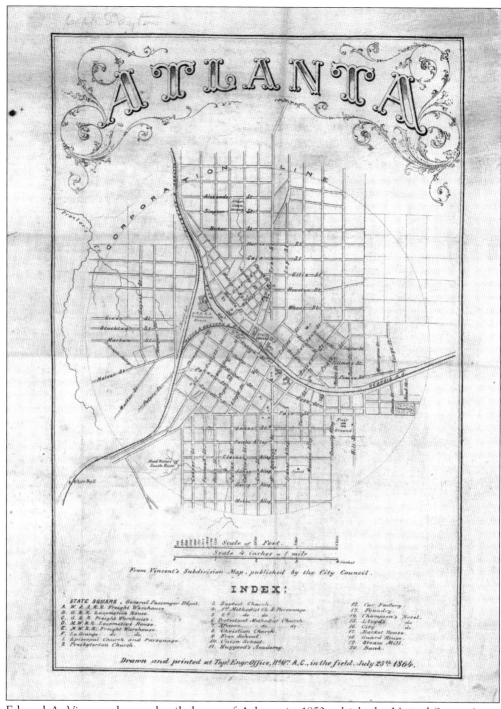

Edward A. Vincent drew a detailed map of Atlanta in 1853, which the United States Army reprinted in this version from 1864. The map clearly shows railroads were the center of Atlanta, and development cropped up around their right-of-ways. In fact, looking at a modern map or aerial view of Atlanta, it is easy to see that this layout more or less remains in place. (Courtesy of the Library of Congress.)

As Atlanta grew, businesses for travelers arose, including the Atlanta Hotel and the Trout House, pictured at right in 1864 and named for owner Jeremiah F. Trout. Confederate president Jefferson Davis, traveling to Montgomery, Alabama, to assume the presidency of the Confederacy, arrived in Atlanta and spoke at the Trout House on February 16, 1861. The Atlanta Hotel is perhaps best remembered as the location where future Confederate States of America vice president Alexander H. Stephens was stabbed during a political argument in 1848. Both hotels burned in November 1864. (Both, courtesy of the Library of Congress.)

One major hotel in Chattanooga was the Crutchfield House, dating to 1847 and situated just feet away from the Union Depot. A reporter for a Tuskegee, Alabama, newspaper in 1859 called the hotel, previously known as the Griffin House, "a tolerably good hotel." (Courtesy of the Library of Congress, Prints & Photographs Division, Civil War Photographs.)

"The hotel swarmed with people arriving and departing with the trains, east, west, north and south, hurrying to and fro with eager and excited looks," a writer with *Harper's New Monthly Magazine* wrote. "Chattanooga is a new place, apparently just cut out of the woods." During the Civil War, the hotel was used as a hospital for injured soldiers. It survived the war but burned in 1867. Shortly thereafter, John T. Read built a new hotel in the same location. (Courtesy of the National Archives.)

KINGSTON, GEORGIA.

While the Western & Atlantic was instrumental in the founding of Atlanta, it was also responsible for the growth of many cities across North Georgia, including Kingston, as illustrated here during the Civil War. In Kingston, the Western & Atlantic interchanged with the 18-mile-long Rome Railroad, chartered as the Memphis Branch Railroad and Steamboat Company of Georgia in 1839. (Courtesy of the Library of Congress.)

Big Shanty, a community that grew around a freshwater spring as workers built the Western & Atlantic roughly two decades earlier, derived its name from a relatively steep grade called the "big grade to the shanties." Aside from the eating house, Big Shanty was the site of Camp MacDonald, a Confederate camp. Artist Alfred R. Waud, in June or July 1864, drew this image depicting water tanks in Big Shanty. (Courtesy of the Library of Congress.)

The Atlanta Hotel, seen in the background of the photograph above from 1864, was one of the first buildings constructed in what was then Marthasville. "Atlanta is a thriving, bustling place—made so by the many Railroads which terminate and cross at that point," a writer in the *Yorkville Enquirer* of South Carolina noted in a May 17, 1855, article. "You can see more engines, [train] cars, depots, work-shops and so-forth, at Atlanta, than in any town or city in the South." (Both, courtesy of the Library of Congress, Prints & Photographs Division, Civil War Photographs.)

Two

THE CIVIL WAR

It was a rainy Saturday morning in April 1862 when a group of suspicious men boarded a northbound Western & Atlantic train at Marietta, Georgia. The men held tickets to varying points along the line, trying to make it seem as though they were not a part of one large group.

As the train wound its way around Kennesaw Mountain, the conductor alerted passengers, "Big Shanty. Twenty Minutes for breakfast!" The train ground to a halt and most passengers disembarked to grab a quick breakfast at the Lacy Hotel, a two-story eating house the Western & Atlantic built in the years before the Civil War.

The men remained in place for a moment, then made their way to the front of the train and made off with the locomotive and three boxcars. Their plan was simple: Destroy the Western & Atlantic between Atlanta and Chattanooga with the hopes of ending of the Civil War. They successfully stole a Southern locomotive—the *General*—deep behind enemy lines, and they did it just feet from the Confederate Camp McDonald.

The raiders did not make it to their planned destination of Chattanooga, and they abandoned the locomotive north of Ringgold, Georgia. While their plan failed, the event, better remembered as the Great Locomotive Chase or the Andrews Raid, is one of the most memorable of the Civil War. Its participants were the first recipients of the Medal of Honor.

The incursion did inflict some level of damage to the Western & Atlantic, but the railroad quickly restored the line and placed it back in service.

"Let this be a warning to the railroad men and every body else in the Confederate States. Let an engine never be left alone a moment," the *Southern Confederacy* wrote in its April 15, 1862, edition. "Let additional guards be placed at our bridges. This is a matter we specially urged in the Confederacy long ago. We hope it will now be heeded."

Except for the Andrews Raid, the Civil War did not come to the Western & Atlantic until 1863 and 1864. But with the start of the war in 1861, it was apparent the fighting would have a dire effect on the railroad, particularly financially. "Of the future of the road, I will only say, that the present prospect is very gloomy, as to its making much money," Supt. John W. Lewis wrote in the September 30, 1861, annual report.

The impact of the war was clearly felt, as Western & Atlantic superintendent John S. Rowland noted in his October 1, 1862, report. The railroad lost 180 cars that were in use on other railroads, and the links with the Western & Atlantic had been severed because of the war. "I trust the Confederate Government will, at the proper time, make good these losses to the Road," Rowland noted optimistically.

"Up to this time, we have been able to keep our motive power in good running order; but the difficulty of getting supplies for our Engine and Machine Shops, of the various kinds absolutely necessary, is now being seriously felt," he added.

A year later, in 1863, Union colonel Abel D. Streight led a raid to destroy the Western & Atlantic. Much like the earlier attempts to destroy the road, this attempt fell short of its objective. The strike ended when Streight's 1,700 men surrendered to Confederate brigadier general Nathan Bedford Forrest and a force of 500 men at Cedar Bluff, Alabama. Later that year, as Confederate troops left Chattanooga, Union forces pursued them into North Georgia, fighting in and around Ringgold and heavily damaging the Western & Atlantic depot there. Confederate soldiers repelled the Union attack, driving them back to Chattanooga.

Despite the failed attempts to destroy the Western & Atlantic, Union general William T. Sherman was determined to succeed and "make Georgia howl." He kicked off his Atlanta campaign in May 1864, essentially marching from Chattanooga to Atlanta following the route of the Western & Atlantic. Fighting in Georgia during 1864 was some of the most intense of the Civil War.

In 1864, the two armies engaged in fights at Resaca, Kennesaw Mountain, Marietta, Smyrna, and Pace's Ferry before the battle and eventual fall of Atlanta.

Sherman later wrote that "every foot" of the Western & Atlantic "should be sacred ground, because it was once moistened by patriotic blood; and that over a hundred miles of it was fought a continuous battle of one hundred and twenty days, during which, day and night, were heard the continuous boom of cannon and the sharp crack of the rifle."

After the fall of Atlanta, Confederate troops under Gen. John Bell Hood marched north toward Nashville. Hoping to break Sherman's supply line, Hood attacked Union troops positioned at Allatoona Pass on October 5, 1864. The battle that ensued is considered by many historians to be one of the Civil War's bloodiest, but it ultimately did not break Union troops' position.

As Sherman prepared to depart Atlanta in November 1864 for his infamous March to the Sea, he ordered the destruction of the railroad buildings in Atlanta, including the car shed.

The US Military Railroad (USMRR) operated the line from September 1, 1864, to September 25, 1865. When the federal government returned the Western & Atlantic to the state, it was "a rough patchwork of damaged and crooked rails, laid on rotten crossties and on rough poles and other make-shifts," historian Ulrich B. Phillips wrote. Additionally, "eight miles of track at the upper end were entirely missing, while the rolling stock was more nearly fit for the scrap heap than for traffic."

About a month before the Great Locomotive Chase, Union general Don Carlos Buell approved a raid against Confederate railroads. Union spy James J. Andrews led a small group of spies to Atlanta, where they were to rendezvous with an engineer who previously agreed to steal a locomotive. The scheme failed because the engineer did not show for the raid. (Courtesy of the Library of Congress.)

Disappointed with his failure in Atlanta, Andrews persuaded Maj. Gen. Ormsby M. Mitchel to authorize a second raid. In April 1862, Andrews returned to Georgia. This time, however, he tapped two dozen men for the mission, including several engineers. The group was delayed by bad weather, and the raid took place on a rainy Saturday, April 12, 1862. (Courtesy of the Library of Congress.)

JAMES J. ANDERWS. Engraved from an old Ambrotype.

Andrews, born around 1829 in Holiday's Cove, Virginia (today Weirton, West Virginia), devised the daring plan. "Boys, I tried this once before and failed; now, I will succeed or leave my bones in Dixie," he told his men before the raid. He was executed in Atlanta on June 7, 1862. (Courtesy of the Library of Congress.)

At 6:00 a.m. on April 12, 1862, the *General* steamed into Big Shanty (today Kennesaw). Passengers disembarked and headed to the Lacy Hotel to grab a 25¢ breakfast that included ham, waffles, grits, gravy, fried chicken, coffee, fresh vegetables, biscuits, and flapjacks with sorghum syrup. George Lacy began leasing the house in 1859 or 1860, giving it the name remembered by history. (Courtesy of HathiTrust.)

Seizing the Train.

In Big Shanty, the raiders stole the *General* and three empty box cars. "For one moment of most intense suspense all was still—then a pull—a jar—a clang—and we were flying away on our perilous journey," raider William Pittenger later wrote in one of several accounts he published chronicling the Great Locomotive Chase. (Courtesy of the Library of Congress.)

CAPTURE OF THE TRAIN IN AN ENEMY'S CAMP.

"This capture was a wonderful triumph," wrote Pittenger, whose 1889 book *The Great Locomotive Chase* featured illustrations bringing the action to life. "To seize a train of cars in an enemy's camp, surrounded by thousands of soldiers, and carry it off without a shot fired or an angry gesture, was a marvelous achievement. There are times when whole years of intense enjoyment seem condensed into a single moment. It was so with us then." (Courtesy of the Library of Congress.)

William A. Fuller, born in 1836 in Morrow Station, south of Atlanta, was the conductor on the northbound passenger train that morning. Much to the amusement of those in Big Shanty, Fuller led a pursuing party, first on foot, then on a pole car, and finally by commandeering a number of locomotives. His dogged pursuit of the "engine thieves," as the Southern press called the raiders, helped save the railroad from total destruction. (Courtesy of the Library of Congress.)

After defeating Confederate forces at Missionary Ridge near Chattanooga in November 1863, Union troops pursued retreating Confederate forces to Ringgold Gap near the Western & Atlantic Railroad pass through Taylor's Ridge. Although Confederate troops under the leadership of Maj. Gen. Patrick Cleburne were greatly outnumbered, they held off Union troops during an intense five-hour fight. The Western & Atlantic Railroad depot was damaged during the battle. (Courtesy of HathiTrust.)

Union officials quickly understood Chattanooga's value as a logistic hub. Here, a US Military Railroad train operates in Chattanooga, likely sometime in 1864. But even after Union troops assumed control of railroads in and around Chattanooga, Confederate forces often sabotaged rail lines in the area. (Courtesy of the Library of Congress.)

After Confederate forces defeated Union troops in Chickamauga, Georgia, the Union retreated to Chattanooga. Confederate general Braxton Bragg led a siege of the city in a bid to cut Union supply lines. Following a series of battles around Chattanooga, Bragg and his Confederate forces retreated from the area on November 26, 1863. (Courtesy of the Library of Congress.)

This photograph was likely taken in 1864 in Chattanooga. The city was nicknamed the "Gateway to the Lower South" and served as the base for Sherman's Atlanta campaign. It shows Confederate prisoners at Union Depot. (Courtesy of the Library of Congress.)

In his October 1, 1862, report, Western & Atlantic superintendent John S. Rowland was relatively optimistic but noted the war took a toll on the line: "Our Rolling Stock of every description has been terribly cut up and much abused, and in many cases almost ruined, in the transportation of troops." (Courtesy of the Library of Congress.)

Because of Atlanta's strategic value as a railroad hub, it quickly became a target for Sherman, who captured the city in September 1864. "So Atlanta is ours and fairly won," Sherman, pictured at right in Atlanta in 1864, famously told officials back in Washington. (Both, courtesy of the Library of Congress.)

In the early morning hours of October 5, 1864, Confederate troops arrived at Allatoona Pass, pictured here in 1864. Confederate general Samuel G. French demanded Union troops surrender "to avoid a needless effusion of blood." French gave his Union counterpart, Gen. John M. Corse, five minutes to decide. (Photograph by Mathew Brady, courtesy of the National Archives.)

General Corse declined French's offer, saying, "We are prepared for the 'needless effusion of blood' whenever it is agreeable to you." The battle that ensued—a Union victory—is considered by many historians to be one of the Civil War's bloodiest fights. (Photograph by George N. Barnard, courtesy of the J. Paul Getty Museum, Los Angeles.)

Thure de Thulstrup, a native of Sweden, depicted the battle in this 1887 painting. The Union side suffered more than 700 casualties, roughly 35 percent of its force at the battle. The Confederate side sustained nearly 900 casualties, roughly 27 percent of its soldiers. (Courtesy of the Library of Congress.)

Artist Alfred R. Waud sketched this view of Tunnel Hill, Georgia, during the Civil War. Waud, a native of London, was a prolific illustrator during and after the Civil War. Many of his works appeared in *Harper's Weekly* and other popular publications of the time. He died in Marietta in 1891 while touring Southern battlefields. (Courtesy of the Library of Congress.)

The October 20, 1864, superintendent's report offered a gloomy view of the state of the railroad. "If our working expenses should appear inordinately heavy, I refer you to the fact, that at the beginning of the year we were almost destitute of the materials necessary for the successful working of the Road," Supt. George. D. Phillips noted. "My present situation is one of difficulty and embarrassment." (Courtesy of the Library of Congress.)

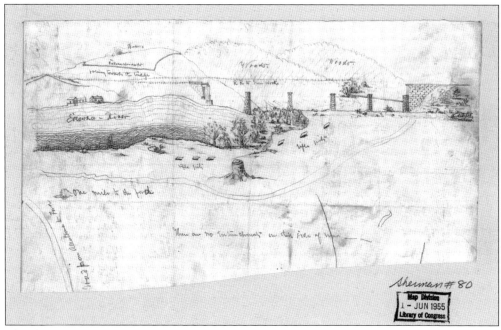

This sketch shows the fortifications near the Etowah River. Retreating Confederate troops burned the bridge in 1864, hoping to slow advancing Union forces. Union troops rebuilt the crossing in a matter of days, restoring their critical rail link. (Courtesy of the Library of Congress.)

In retreating from Atlanta, Gen. John Bell Hood attached several locomotives, including the *General*, to the front of an 81-car train in an unsuccessful attempt to remove supplies from Atlanta. On the night of September 1, 1864, Hood ordered the destruction of the train as it stood in front of the Schoefield and Markham Rolling Mill in Atlanta. The aftermath is memorialized in the photograph above. Mathew Brady captured this iconic image of the "hero locomotive," the *General*, in Atlanta following the blast. After the war, the Western & Atlantic repaired the *General* and returned it to service. (Above, courtesy of the Library of Congress; right, courtesy of National Archives.)

Atlanta fell to the Union on September 2, 1864. Sherman and his forces remained in the city for two months. "The foundries, furnaces, rolling-mills, machine shops, laboratories and railroad repair-shops . . . which have been accumulated at Atlanta, are ours now," reported the *New York Times*. (Courtesy of the Library of Congress, Prints & Photographs Division, Civil War Photographs.)

Famed Civil War–era photographer George N. Barnard took this photograph of Atlanta in October 1864 from the cupola of the Female Seminary shortly before the burning of the city. The car shed is visible at center, but its days were limited. (Courtesy of the Library of Congress, Prints & Photographs Division, Civil War Photographs.)

Sherman ordered the destruction of Atlanta's Union Station before leaving the city on his March to the Sea. The resulting scene Barnard captured perfectly illustrates a famous Sherman quote: "You cannot qualify war in harsher terms than I will. War is cruelty and you cannot refine it, and those who brought war into our country deserve all the curses and maledictions a people can pour out." On November 15, 1864, Sherman set off on his infamous March to the Sea, which culminated with the taking of the port city of Savannah. (Both, courtesy of the Library of Congress.)

UNITED STATES MILITARY RAILROADS:
Division of the Mississippi.
CHATTANOOGA & ATLANTA LINE.
Time Table No. 3.

Takes Effect Monday, Aug. 15th, 1864, at 2:30 O'Clock A. M.

Trains from the Front			Distances between Stations	STATIONS.	Distances from Chattanooga	Trains toward the Front.		
No. 6.	No. 4.	No. 2.				No. 1.	No. 3.	No. 5.
10 45 A.M.	1 50 A.M.	4 45 P.M.	0	Ar. Chattanooga, Dep.	0	2 50 A.M.	9 00 A.M.	6 10 P.M.
10 00	1 10	4 00	6	**Junction,**	6	3 50	**10 00**	7 10
9 35	12 55	3 45	2	Chicamauga,	8	4 05	10 15	7 25
8 50	12 10 A.M.	3 00	8	Graysville,	16	4 50	11 00	8 10
8 20	11 40 P.M.	2 30	5	Ringgold,	21	5 20	11 30 A.M.	8 40
7 35	10 55	1 45	8	Tunnel Hill,	29	6 05	12 15 P.M.	9 28
6 50	**10 10**	**1 00 P.M.**	7	**Dalton,**	36	**6 50**	**1 00**	**10 10**
5 50	8 45	12 00 M.	9	Tilton,	45	7 45	1 55	11 05
5 05	8 00	11 20 A.M.	7	Resaca,	52	8 30	2 40	11 50 P.M.
4 30	7 25	10 50	6	Calhoun,	58	9 05	3 15	12 25 A.M.
3 55	6 30	**10 00**	9	**Adairsville,**	67	**10 00**	4 10	1 20
2 30	**5 30**	8 55	10	**Kingston,**	77	11 10	**5 30**	**2 30**
1 30	4 35	8 00	7	Cass,	84	11 55 A.M.	6 15	3 15
1 10	4 20	7 45	2½	Rogers,	86½	12 10 P.M.	6 30	3 30
12 52	4 05	7 30	2½	Cartersville,	89	12 25	6 45	3 45
12 38	3 50	7 18	2	Etowah,	91	12 40	7 00	4 00
12 18 A.M.	3 32	7 00	3	Easton,	94	1 00	7 20	4 18
12 00 M.	3 20	6 48	2	Allatoona,	96	1 15	7 35	4 30
11 30 P.M.	2 55	6 18	5	Acworth,	101	1 45	8 10	5 00
10 55	**2 25**	**5 45**	6	**Big Shanty,**	107	**2 25**	8 50	**5 45**
10 00	1 25	4 40	9	**Marietta,**	116	3 20	**10 00**	6 35
9 25	12 55	4 05	4	Ruffs,	120	3 45	10 25	7 00
8 50	12 30 P.M.	3 35	5	Vinings,	125	4 15	10 55	7 30
7 50 P.M.	11 30 A.M.	2 30 A.M.	11	Dep. Atlanta, Ar.	136	5 15 P.M.	11 55 P.M.	8 30 A.M.

SPECIAL INSTRUCTIONS.

1st. The running of Trains by this Time Table will be governed by the book of "General Rules" of the General Superintendent, issued March 31st, 1864, except as to General Rule No. 5.

2d. General Rule No. 5, is abandoned during the continuance of this Time Table. After Trains moving "towards the front" become irregular by loosing the hour allowed them, Trains "from the front" will have the absolute right of Track, and all other Trains must be kept entirely out of their way.

3d. Trains of the C. & K. Line will have the same rights to run between Chattanooga and Junction as Trains of this Line.

4th. When Trains meet they must always stop long enough for Conductors to exchange communications, and furnish each other with all necessary information in regard to trains following them.

5th. Have your trains under perfect control approaching the Tennessee Depot at Chattanooga.

6th. Consult the Bulletin Boards daily, and note all new orders.

7th. Conductors and Brakemen will, as far as practicable, notice the condition of Telegraph wires, and when down, report to the Section Foreman and first Telegraph Office.

W. C. TAYLOR, Superintendent.

APPROVED:

A. ANDERSON, Gen. Sup't Gov't R. R'ds, Mil. Div. of the Miss.

U. S. MIL. R. R. Printing Office, Nashville, Tenn.

The United States War Department created the US Military Railroad to operate railroads it seized during the Civil War. This timetable from 1864 shows trains operating on the Western & Atlantic both "from the Front" and "toward the Front" and making seemingly all stops between Atlanta and Chattanooga. (Courtesy of Duke University.)

Three

REBUILDING THE ROAD

When the federal government returned the Western & Atlantic to the State of Georgia following the Civil War, it was in rather poor shape.

"The Western & Atlantic R. R. has been restored to the State authorities in a dilapidated condition; its track and bridges hastily and insufficiently repaired for temporary use; many of the buildings appurtenant to it, and especially to its successful operation, destroyed, and the rolling stock reduced far below the exigencies of the service," said Georgia governor Charles J. Jenkins in his inaugural address.

Workers replaced 296,812 crossties along the line, which was nearly every crosstie between Atlanta and Chattanooga. The railroad rebuilt depots destroyed or heavily damaged during the war, including those in Marietta, Acworth, Etowah, Cartersville, Tilton, Tunnel Hill, and Chickamauga. The state also purchased new rolling stock and eight 4-4-0 locomotives from the federal government for use on the line.

However, "there was a general feeling among the officials of the road that in its sale of locomotives and cars to the State, the United States Government had not given the Western and Atlantic Railroad the same consideration as other Southern railroads had received when equipment and supplies were sold," James Houstoun Johnston wrote.

In July 1868, Rufus Bullock, a New York native who served as Georgia's governor from 1868 until 1871, removed the Western & Atlantic's leadership and installed his own team: Col. Ed Hulburt as superintendent, A.L. "Fatty" Harris as a supervisor, and Foster Blodgett as treasurer. In 1870, Bullock elevated Blodgett to the superintendent's post, and Blodgett allegedly said he took the role to manage the railroad's "public and political policy."

This era is marked with allegations of fraud, primarily involving Bullock and businessman Hannibal I. Kimball, a man either forgotten or ill-regarded by historians. Of Kimball, historian John F. Stover once wrote he "seemed to see nothing wrong in selling the cars without bothering to complete delivery."

But Kimball played a huge role in shaping postwar Atlanta. In 1866, he and George M. Pullman established sleeping car lines in the South. He also financed the 45-mile-long Cartersville & Van Wert Railroad, which fed into the Western & Atlantic in Cartersville. In October 1870, Kimball opened Kimball House, a landmark hotel situated in the heart of Atlanta and adjacent to Union Station, which opened in 1871.

During this time, hundreds of Western & Atlantic employees, including William A. Fuller, the conductor who successfully chased down Union spies during the Civil War, were dismissed from the railroad. Blodgett replaced them with people loyal to him. Perhaps the most telling story from this era involves N.P. Hotchkiss, the railroad's auditor. When asked how he saved $20,000 or $30,000 in just a few years while making a salary of $2,000, he merely responded, "By the exercise of the most rigid economy."

As a result of the allegations of corruption, by the fall of 1870 the Western & Atlantic had fallen again into a pitiful condition. "Blodgett was robbing the road of all it was earning and of all he could borrow in its name, and now demanded an appropriation of $500,000 from the State for repairs," James Houstoun Johnston wrote. "As an alternative he proposed that the State should lease the road to some of its citizens. The condition of things had now become intolerable to the people, and a great cry arose for the road to be taken out of politics."

On December 27, 1870, the state leased the line for $25,000 per month for a period of 20 years to a group of investors that included Joseph E. Brown, governor of the state during the Civil War. He resigned as chief justice of the Supreme Court of Georgia before submitting a bid, and was subsequently named president of the railroad. But even the lease was not without controversy. Other bidders sought to lease the line for more money. Bullock disregarded the higher bids, and despite the hullabaloo, the bid from Brown and his associates stood.

In 1870, the four lines serving Atlanta—the Atlanta & West Point, the Georgia, the Macon & Western, and the Western & Atlantic—agreed to build a new Union Depot in Atlanta's State Square to replace a temporary depot the railroad had used since about 1868.

The new station opened in 1871, the year Bullock and Kimball left Georgia. During this era, Western & Atlantic officials acquired coal-burning locomotives. They also converted other locomotives, including the famous *General* and *Texas* steamers, from wood burners to coal burners.

The Western & Atlantic's role in shaping communities along its line is perfectly illustrated in Smyrna. During the 1830s and 1840s, the railroad attracted workers to settle in the area. In 1872, when the State of Georgia incorporated Smyrna, named in honor of one of Paul the Apostle's seven churches in Asia, it named John C. Moore, a conductor on the Western & Atlantic, the city's first mayor, a position then known as intendant.

On May 31 and June 1, 1886, workers changed the gauge of the railroad from five feet to four feet, nine inches, making it compliant with the new nationwide standard gauge of four feet, eight and a half inches. The railroad stopped all traffic on the line while the change was made between Atlanta and Chattanooga. "In effecting the change, four men to the mile will be employed, with one foreman to the section," the *Atlanta Constitution* reported. By this time, the railroad had already re-gauged 500 cars and 34 locomotives. Another change came in 1890 when the railroad stopped naming locomotives.

The Joseph Brown era ended on December 27, 1890, when the state leased the line for $35,001 per month for 29 years to the Nashville, Chattanooga & St. Louis Railway, chartered in December 1845 as the Nashville & Chattanooga. To win the lease, the railroad outbid the Richmond and West Point Terminal and Warehouse Company, which proposed a $35,000 monthly lease, prompting claims of collusion.

Upon leasing the line, the Nashville, Chattanooga & St. Louis went to work upgrading the line, which again had fallen into some level of disrepair during the previous lease. The company spent more than $400,000 on upgrades during the first 18 months of operation, including new steel rails, side tracks, iron bridges, and crossties.

Following the Civil War, the Western & Atlantic used a temporary depot in Atlanta but quickly outgrew the facility. Belgian-American architect Max Corput, a partner in the Corput and Bass firm, designed the city's new Union Station, which opened in 1871 and served Atlanta until 1930. At that time, it was razed and replaced by a new station. (Courtesy of Railfanning.org.)

Union Station, located on the site of the antebellum car shed, was one of more than 400 buildings erected in Atlanta in 1871. While much of the South remained devastated in the wake of the Civil War, the building boom symbolized Atlanta's progress. (Courtesy of the New York Public Library.)

The bridge over the Chattahoochee River, depicted in this c. 1910 postcard, was destroyed and rebuilt during the Civil War. Even after the war, the crossing was not safe from Mother Nature; in December 1865, heavy rains caused the river to rise. Debris then crashed into the bridge, taking trestles with it. The bridge was repaired and returned to service by the end of January 1866. (Courtesy of Railfanning.org.)

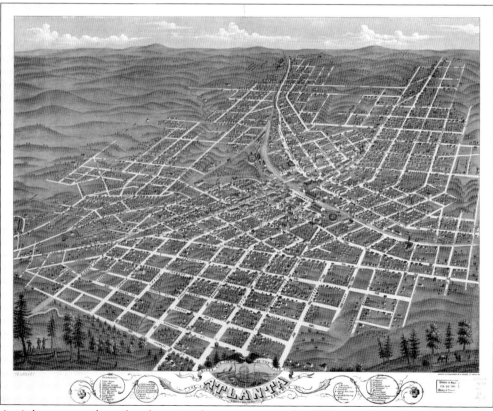

As Atlanta grew, the railroad remained at its center, as this 1871 map shows. By 1877, morning trains departed Atlanta for destinations such as Chicago, Cincinnati, Louisville, and Little Rock, Arkansas. The railroad also established in-state runs such as the Rome Express between Atlanta and Rome, Georgia. (Courtesy of the Library of Congress.)

In many ways, Atlanta flourished during Reconstruction, and by 1870, the city had grown to more than 21,700 residents. This explosive growth transformed the "Gate City" into a major economic engine that continues to this day. Artist Horace Bradley created this wood engraving depicting the commercial heart of Atlanta; it appeared in *Harper's Weekly* on February 12, 1887. (Courtesy of Wikimedia Commons.)

Rufus Bullock served as the 46th governor of Georgia. The New York native moved to Augusta, Georgia, in 1857 for his job with the Adams Express telegraph company. He opposed secession, but despite his views, he rose to the rank of lieutenant colonel in the Confederate army. He entered politics after the Civil War and was elected governor in April 1868, defeating the heavily favored Democrat, John B. Gordon. For his part, Gordon probably went on to head the Ku Klux Klan in Georgia. (Courtesy of the Library of Congress.)

Hannibal I. Kimball played an enormous role in shaping post–Civil War Atlanta. He helped convince Georgia legislators to make Atlanta the state capital and built two landmark hotels downtown. He also bought the land for the new Union Depot built in 1871 and constructed tracks along Alabama Street, which resulted in a new warehouse district along the thoroughfare. (Courtesy of HathiTrust.)

Kimball opened the first Kimball House hotel on October 17, 1870, on the site of the antebellum Atlanta Hotel. The new hotel was still under construction at the time of its opening but was completed shortly thereafter. The hotel had a short life and burned in August 1883. (Courtesy of Wikimedia Commons.)

After the 1883 fire, Atlanta civic leaders, including George Adair, Henry W. Grady, and Richard Peters, urged Kimball, who then lived in Chicago, to rebuild the famed structure. The second Kimball House, built to be fireproof, opened on January 1, 1885. It was razed in 1959 and replaced with a parking deck. (Courtesy of Wikimedia Commons.)

When the Western & Atlantic surveyed and subsequently built its line, the route bypassed the town of Cassville. At the time, Cassville was the county seat of Cass County (today named Bartow County). Cass Station, seen here around 1875, was built in 1857 about two miles from the city proper. (Courtesy of the Bartow History Museum.)

Legend says residents of Cassville did not want the railroad to pass through their community, which was one of the largest in North Georgia before the Civil War. At some point, they reconsidered and asked the railroad to reroute its line through town. The railroad offered to redirect the line if residents paid for a new survey and construction, but it did not happen. (Courtesy of the Bartow History Museum.)

Cassville was largely destroyed during the Civil War. The town was not rebuilt, and following the war, much of Bartow County's business relocated to Cartersville, the new county seat. However, after the war, the Cass Station train depot remained in service and stood until it apparently burned in or after 1969. (Courtesy of the Adairsville Depot History Museum and Welcome Center.)

The Western & Atlantic was a lifeline for residents in communities up and down the line. A one-story brick depot was built in 1852–1853 in Calhoun. "Calhoun has a good depot and everybody is satisfied with the service the new lessees are giving us," noted the *Calhoun Times* (as printed in the *Atlanta Constitution*) in 1891. (Courtesy of the Adairsville Depot History Museum and Welcome Center.)

After the Civil War, the Western & Atlantic rebuilt many of the depots along the line, including the one at Ringgold, pictured here around 1904. The depot, built in 1849 with 14-inch dark sandstone walls, was heavily damaged in 1863 and repaired with lighter limestone blocks, repairs that are readily visible today. (Courtesy of HathiTrust.)

The railroad's upgrades were not limited to the Atlanta end of the line. In Chattanooga, the railroad expanded Union Depot in the 1880s with the addition of a new headhouse and a new freight building. In 1927, a portion of the car shed was torn down and replaced with butterfly sheds. (Courtesy of the Chattanooga Public Library.)

WAR SCENES

Views
....AND **Pointers**

·······ON·······

W. & A. R. R.

....AND....

N. C. & St. L. Ry.

ɔpliments...
PASSENGER DEPARTMENT,
_____W. & A. R. R.

In the decades following the war, the Western & Atlantic marketed its line as a way for tourists to visit North Georgia's Civil War battlefields and produced travel brochures such as this one for its passengers. The line's "scenery will fully repay every lover of nature's beauty and sublimity," wrote Gen. William T. Sherman in one version of the pamphlet. (Courtesy of HathiTrust.)

Philadelphia-based Baldwin Locomotive Works built the *Acworth*, a 4-6-0, for the Western & Atlantic in 1881. When the 1870 lease neared its expiration in 1890, Joseph E. Brown and his partners were only required to return the 44 locomotives (plus a scrapped one) to the State of Georgia. The Acworth, like many other Western & Atlantic locomotives, was sold to the Plant System railroad. (Courtesy of HathiTrust.)

In many ways, the *General* served as an ambassador for the Western & Atlantic, traveling to a number of reunions, worlds' fairs, and other such gatherings, including the August 1888 annual encampment of the Grand Army of the Republic in Columbus, Ohio. The *General* traveled to Columbus under its own steam, and conductor William Fuller gave a talk about the raid, then paid tribute to the raiders. (Courtesy of HathiTrust.)

On May 31 and June 1, 1886, railroad workers re-gauged the Western & Atlantic from five feet to a width of four feet, nine inches, compatible with the new national gauge of four feet, eight and a half inches. The railroad stopped traffic on the line while the change was made between Atlanta and Chattanooga, where this photograph was taken. (Courtesy of the New York Public Library.)

On April 13, 1887, the Western & Atlantic offered an excursion from Chattanooga to Atlanta for the families of the members of the International Association of Car Accountants. The famous *General* locomotive pulled the train, and when it reached Allatoona Pass, the group disembarked for a photograph. (Courtesy of Georgia Archives, Vanishing Georgia Collection, brt138-91.)

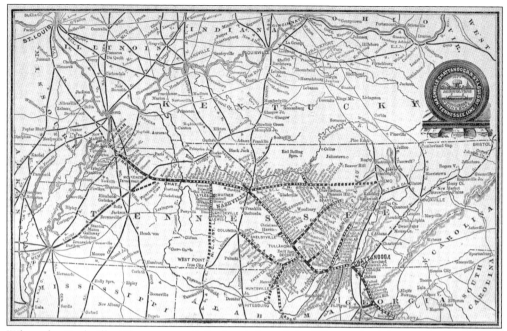

When the Nashville, Chattanooga & St. Louis leased the Western & Atlantic, the line joined a much larger network, as evidenced by this 1891 map from *Poor's Manual of the Railroads of the United States*. As of June 30, 1890, the Nashville, Chattanooga & St. Louis had 109 locomotives that operated across a rail network of more than 652 miles. (Courtesy of Wikimedia Commons.)

The *General* continued to travel to many reunions and fairs during the waning years of the 19th century, including the Chicago World's Fair in 1893 and the Cotton States and International Exposition in Atlanta in 1895. Here, conductor William A. Fuller poses next to the venerable locomotive during the 1895 Atlanta exposition. (Courtesy of HathiTrust.)

The area around Union Station was dangerous, particularly for pedestrians. In 1901, the *Atlanta Constitution* noted: "There is only just room enough in the shed for truck-men and switch engines, but there is little provision for the traveling public, and it is a case of every man for himself. . . . Pandemonium reigns." (Courtesy of the New York Public Library.)

Union Station was heralded as a majestic structure when it opened, but public opinion turned against the building. One strange happening dates to 1901, when a foot-and-a-half-long live alligator was found in the waiting room. Once word spread about the exotic find, armed men descended on the station "dodging in and out of the dark recesses looking for freak specimens" before being ushered out of the depot, the *Atlanta Constitution* reported. (Courtesy of the New York Public Library.)

Four

DAWN OF THE 20TH CENTURY

The first half of the 20th century in many ways was an era of transition for the Western & Atlantic, moving the line from a Civil War–era railroad to the modern line of today.

The Nashville, Chattanooga & St. Louis, which started leasing the line in 1890, upgraded the road in anticipation of additional traffic. The Louisville & Nashville, which gained a controlling interest of the Nashville, Chattanooga & St. Louis in 1880, owned lines that fed into the Western & Atlantic in Cartersville and Marietta. To reach Atlanta, it looked as though the Louisville & Nashville might build a competing line paralleling the Western & Atlantic from north of Cartersville to Atlanta.

Such a move would likely diminish the value of the Western & Atlantic. As a result, Georgia lawmakers responded with a new law preventing the issuance "of any corporate power to any private company to parallel the tracks of the Western & Atlantic Railway, so long as the same is the property of the State." Ultimately, the Louisville & Nashville used the Western & Atlantic as its gateway to Atlanta. The state Supreme Court later ruled the law unconstitutional.

But even as the region and the Western & Atlantic moved into the modern era, some dangers did still exist, as evidenced by a brazen robbery on January 16, 1914, that seemed better fit for the Wild West. A well-dressed man boarded the southbound train in Vinings and made his way to the parlor car. Wielding a revolver, he asked passengers to hand over their money. A police officer on the train confronted the robber on the coach's rear platform, and the two exchanged gunfire. The robber laughed and dropped from the train, making off with about $280. Authorities later arrested the man near where he fell from the train, apparently walking toward Atlanta.

Shortly thereafter, in February 1917, the state and the Nashville, Chattanooga & St. Louis agreed to a 50-year renewal of the lease. Under the new accord, the railroad agreed to pay a total rent of $27 million (or $45,000 per month) and make at least $3 million in improvements. (The lease renewal actually did not go into effect until December 27, 1919.)

Then the United States entered World War I. Following an act of Congress, the federal government took control of the nation's railroads on December 28, 1917. The action had little practical effect on the Western & Atlantic. Between Dalton and Phelps, five miles to the south, the Western & Atlantic paralleled the Southern Railway. The feds installed switches and ran the section as a double-track line for both the Southern and Western & Atlantic. The United States Railroad Administration maintained operations until March 1, 1920, when railroads nationwide returned to their owners.

But during this period, the Western & Atlantic was not without controversy, particularly in Chattanooga. For years, city officials there contended the railroad used a nearly 12-acre tract of land owned by the State of Georgia in such a way that hindered growth in Chattanooga.

Even though the state leased the line, state officials regularly inspected the road. "Based on a personal inspection of the Western & Atlantic railroad . . . it is the opinion of the commission that the road-bed is in the best condition at any time in its history," the *Atlanta Constitution* quoted James A. Perry, chairman of the Georgia Public Service Commission, as saying in May 1928.

Between 1919 and 1930, the Nashville, Chattanooga & St. Louis spent more than $2.5 million on upgrades, including a significant portion on increasing the weight of the rail in use. In 1928, the railroad had 55 miles of the heavier 110-pound rail (a section of rail weighing 110 pounds per linear yard), while the remainder of the line had lighter 90-pound rail.

Shortly after Perry's inspection, one of the biggest upgrades on the line was put into service. On December 17, 1928, officials from the Nashville, Chattanooga & St. Louis and the State of Georgia formally opened a new, larger tunnel through Chetoogeta Mountain in Tunnel Hill. "The old tunnel . . . although not constructed in accordance with present engineering standards has, with proper care, stood the test of time and use for about 80 years," the *Atlanta Constitution* quoted Pres. J.B. Hill as saying during a ceremony for the new tunnel. "What progress in our civilization and industrial welfare could be told in the development of transportation alone as reflected in the improvements in train make-up and service now." He added, "No more important thing has occurred to the Western and Atlantic railroad than the building of the new tunnel, which is being opened to traffic today."

Upgrades up and down the line continued, and less than two years after opening the new tunnel, the railroad, on April 18, 1930, opened a new Union Station in Atlanta. It replaced a structure that had been used since just after the Civil War. The 1870s-era station was much maligned during its lifetime, and in 1905, several railroads—the Southern Railway, Seaboard Air Line, Central of Georgia, and the Atlanta & West Point—moved to the new Terminal Station. When the new Union Station opened, it also served the Georgia and Atlantic Coast Line railroads in Atlanta.

During the 1940s, the Nashville, Chattanooga & St. Louis continued to upgrade the Western & Atlantic, spending millions on improvements. These enhancements were driven by growth in industry in the state and the construction of Allatoona Dam, which created Lake Allatoona. Improvements included a new bridge over the Etowah River, centralized traffic control, and the reduction of curves. The railroad also realigned tracks between Acworth and Cartersville. This new alignment formally opened on June 10, 1949, when the *Dixie Flyer* passenger train between Chicago and Florida passed over the line. A slew of railroad dignitaries, including Nashville, Chattanooga & St. Louis president W.S. Hackworth—witnessed the opening.

Even after the Nashville, Chattanooga & St. Louis leased the line, it continued to use the Western & Atlantic name and logo, as this advertisement from the *Walker County Messenger* newspaper in April 1902 shows. The railroad advertised its trains connecting Atlanta with a number of destinations, including Chicago, Cincinnati, Louisville, and St. Louis. (Courtesy of the Digital Library of Georgia.)

With the Nashville, Chattanooga & St. Louis and the Louisville & Nashville sharing tracks between Cartersville and Atlanta, traffic on the Western & Atlantic increased. In 1905, the Nashville, Chattanooga & St. Louis installed a block signal system, allowing for the safer operation of additional trains on the line between Atlanta and Cartersville, where this photograph was taken in 1910. (Courtesy of the Bartow History Museum.)

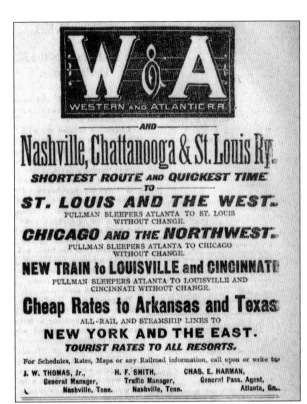

Cartersville, seen here around 1910, replaced Cassville as the Bartow County seat. A Bartow County grand jury in February 1907 recommended a plan to double-track the line between Cartersville and Atlanta. At the time, 22 passenger trains, in addition to many freight trains, operated over the tracks that "greatly endanger the lives of passengers and train crews," reported the *Atlanta Constitution* at the time. (Courtesy of the Bartow History Museum.)

After Methodist revivalist preacher Samuel Porter Jones's death in October 1906, a special train furnished by Nashville, Chattanooga & St. Louis president John Thomas brought his body back to his hometown of Cartersville. "The arrival of the special found practically the whole population of Cartersville assembled about the depot," the *Atlanta Constitution* reported. Following the funeral, Jones's body was taken to Atlanta to lie in state at the Georgia State Capitol. (Courtesy of the Bartow History Museum.)

On June 12, 1912, approximately 100 passengers were on an excursion train from Calhoun to Chattanooga for a picnic when the train derailed in the Willowdale community, near Dalton. Reports at the time indicate three people were killed in the wreck: the train's fireman, a section employee, and a porter. (Courtesy of Georgia Archives, Vanishing Georgia Collection, gor428.)

Western & Atlantic No. 179 is seen here near Dalton pulling an excursion train on June 12, 1912. By this time, the Nashville, Chattanooga & St. Louis purchased larger locomotives, replacing many of the original Western & Atlantic locomotives it acquired in the 1890 lease. (Courtesy of Georgia Archives, Vanishing Georgia Collection, gor426.)

While passenger operations were perhaps the most visible aspect of the Western & Atlantic's operations, it represented just a small percentage of the railroad's business. In the fiscal year ending June 30, 1912, freight accounted for more than 70 percent of the Western & Atlantic's revenues. Passenger operations accounted for 19 percent of revenue, with the balance coming from mail and other operations. (Courtesy of the Bartow History Museum.)

Two men pose in front of a Western & Atlantic locomotive in Marietta around 1915. In July 1915, leaders in Cobb County formally protested a proposed law that would have prohibited the development of a railroad paralleling the Western & Atlantic, saying North Georgia "would be disastrously affected" by such a law. (Courtesy of Georgia Archives, Vanishing Georgia Collection, cob342.)

Kingston, pictured here around 1918, was an important railroad crossroads starting soon after the completion of the Western & Atlantic. The Nashville, Chattanooga & St. Louis acquired the 18-mile-long Rome Railroad in 1896. Kingston remained a railroad junction until October 1943, when the Interstate Commerce Commission (ICC) approved the Nashville, Chattanooga & St. Louis's plan to abandon the line. (Courtesy of the Bartow History Museum.)

Kingston's first depot was built before the Civil War, and Sherman's troops destroyed it in 1864. A second depot, built around 1870, burned in December 1892. The third depot, pictured here, burned in July 1974. Its foundations are still visible today adjacent to the railroad tracks in downtown Kingston. (Courtesy of the Adairsville Depot History Museum and Welcome Center.)

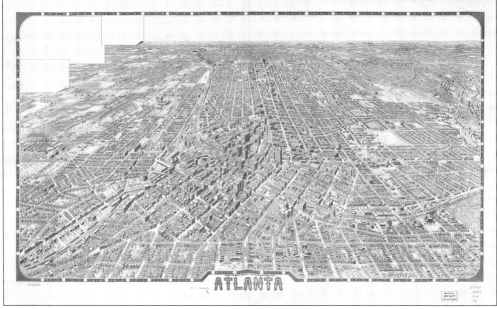

As Atlanta's population grew, railroads remained at the center of the city, as evidenced by this 1919 map of the city. A proposal in July 1919 would have authorized the state's railroad commission to explore extending the Western & Atlantic to the sea, possibly at St. Marys. The proposal went nowhere. Later that year, on December 28, 1919, the Nashville, Chattanooga & St. Louis's new 50-year lease went into effect. (Courtesy of the Library of Congress.)

In addition to the commercial advantages of the railroad, it was also a major employer. According to a January 1923 article in a Cartersville newspaper, the Nashville, Chattanooga & St. Louis employed nearly 10,000 people, paying them a combined $1 million per month. Here, railroad workers pose in front of a caboose in Adairsville. (Courtesy of the Adairsville Depot History Museum and Welcome Center.)

When the railroad built through Adairsville, local landowner William Watts deeded tracts to the railroad. In addition to the depot, the city was also home to a water tower, allowing crews to replenish their locomotives. The railroad helped Adairsville prosper and earn its nickname as the "Granary of the State." (Courtesy of the Adairsville Depot History Museum and Welcome Center.)

Section crews, such as this one photographed in front of the Emerson depot in the 1920s, were vital to maintaining the line. In 1925, the Nashville, Chattanooga & St. Louis spent more than $597,000 for "additions and betterments" and more than $1.2 million during the previous six years, according to a newspaper account. (Courtesy of the Bartow History Museum.)

By the 1930s, when this picture was taken, Cartersville had grown into a respectable industrial center in large part due to its railroad connections. Connecting lines included the Cartersville & Van Wert. The Louisville & Nashville also opened a line between the Cartersville and Etowah, Tennessee, bypassing its Etowah Old Line between Marietta and Etowah, Tennessee. (Courtesy of the Bartow History Museum.)

By the early 20th century, locomotives were much larger than their Civil War predecessors such as the *General*, as seen here. The famed Civil War steamer poses next to locomotive No. 565, a class J2 4-8-4 built by ALCO in 1930. (Courtesy of the Chattanooga Public Library.)

By the 1920s, the antebellum tunnel through Chetoogeta Mountain was too small for the increasingly larger trains in use on the Western & Atlantic. The Nashville, Chattanooga & St. Louis built a larger tunnel to accommodate these trains. The new tunnel is located a few dozen feet away from the older structure. (Courtesy of HathiTrust.)

In December 1928, the Nashville, Chattanooga & St. Louis opened a larger tunnel and deeded it to the state. Here, locomotive No. 581 pulls train No. 94, the *Dixie Flyer*, through the new tunnel on April 17, 1948. The older tunnel is visible on the right. (Courtesy of the Southern Museum of Civil War & Locomotive History Archives, David Salter Collection.)

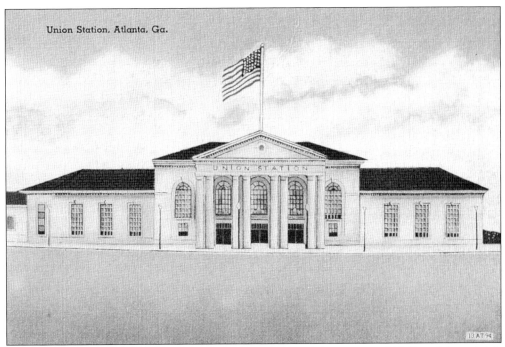

The new Union Depot in Atlanta opened in April 1930. Atlanta mayor I.N. Ragsdale and A.J. Woodruff, vice chairman of the Georgia Public Service Commission, were among the dignitaries to greet a train carrying a private car with Nashville, Chattanooga & St. Louis president J.B. Hill and the railroad's board of directors. Dignitaries then attended a luncheon at East Lake Country Club and a dinner at the Atlanta Athletic Club. After the new station opened, Atlanta building inspector C.J. Bowen issued a permit to raze the old Union Station structure erected in 1871. (Both, courtesy of Railfanning.org.)

prised if Lawrence walks in on you some day for he is talking of going to St. Louis some ... Sundays & he said he was sure going ... to see you. E. M. S.

John T. Read opened the popular Read House hotel, pictured above in a c. 1907 postcard, in 1872 on the site of the former Crutchfield House, next to Chattanooga's Union Depot. The second, and current, Read House opened in the same location in 1926. Many dignitaries, including Winston Churchill, have stayed at the hotel over the years. The building underwent an extensive renovation in 2017–2018. (Above, courtesy of Railfanning.org; below, courtesy of the Tichnor Brothers Collection, Boston Public Library.)

Read House, Chattanooga, Tenn.

The Western & Atlantic helped spur industrial development across North Georgia both before and after the Civil War. Glover Machine Works was one of the industries that grew up along the railroad in Marietta. Between 1902 and 1930, Glover produced more than 200 locomotives. The company's locomotives were often smaller than those built by Baldwin or other famous builders. Today, there are few remnants of this fascinating locomotive builder. Its historic 11-acre campus in Marietta, where the company moved in 1903, was razed in 1995. (Both, courtesy of the Library of Congress.)

Locomotive Nos. 575 and 578 wait to depart Atlanta's Union Station in 1948 for northbound passenger runs. The Nashville, Chattanooga & St. Louis phased out its steam locomotives by the early 1950s. (Courtesy of the Southern Museum of Civil War & Locomotive History Archives, David Salter Collection.)

Dangerous railroad crossings prompted Atlanta officials to build a series of bridges, viaducts, and public plazas atop the tracks. The first bridge over the Western & Atlantic appeared as early as 1852. In August 1921, the state authorized the city of Atlanta to build the Spring Street viaduct, depicted in this postcard. (Courtesy of Railfanning.org.)

Despite numerous safety upgrades, railroading remained dangerous. In July 1940, a northbound Louisville & Nashville freight train collided with a switch engine near Cartersville, killing two engineers, J.O. Greenwell and L.L. Gilstrap, and injuring more than two dozen. The collision caused tank cars to explode, showering onlookers with gasoline. (Courtesy of the Bartow History Museum.)

As part of its realignment in the 1940s, the Nashville, Chattanooga & St. Louis opened a new bridge across the Etowah River. The bridge replaced a structure that incorporated piers built before the Civil War. Here, locomotive No. 580 leads a freight train across the new bridge. (Courtesy of the Southern Museum of Civil War & Locomotive History Archives, David Salter Collection.)

Five

THE DIESEL ERA

In some ways, the post–World War II era was the busiest period in the Western & Atlantic's history—at least from a legal standpoint. It began when the railroad was under the control of the Nashville, Chattanooga & St. Louis, and it culminated with the line as part of CSX, one of the country's largest freight railroads. In between, the railroad was the subject of a pair of lease negotiations, including one that was arguably as hotly contested as the 1890 discussion.

In November 1946, the Nashville, Chattanooga & St. Louis and the Louisville & Nashville jointly ushered in a new era when they introduced the *Georgian*, a diesel-powered streamliner running between St. Louis and Atlanta. Before the first train departed Atlanta, Mildred Delany Slemons Arnall, the wife of former Georgia governor Ellis Arnall, broke a bottle of champagne over the train's nose during a ceremony that included Atlanta mayor William B. Hartsfield and Nashville, Chattanooga & St. Louis president W.S. Hackworth. The train was scheduled to complete the 612-mile trip in 12 hours and 52 minutes, an average speed of approximately 47.5 miles per hour. The train's "streamlined beauty encompasses the most modern of conveniences, offering real comfort and without premium prices," the *Atlanta Constitution* reported.

A decade later, in 1957, the Nashville, Chattanooga & St. Louis merged with the larger Louisville & Nashville, which had had a controlling interest in the former road since 1880. With this action, the Louisville & Nashville assumed the lease of the Western & Atlantic, which would come up for renewal a decade later.

Much like the Nashville, Chattanooga & St. Louis, the Louisville & Nashville used the venerable *General* locomotive for marketing purposes. The biggest opportunity came in 1962 with the centennial of the Great Locomotive Chase. The Louisville & Nashville removed the *General* from its resting place in Chattanooga's Union depot and restored it to running condition. The railroad sent the steamer on a tour that included retracing the route of the famed Civil War episode.

The following year, in advance of a new lease, the state hired a New York engineering firm to help determine the value of the line. In December 1966, the state accepted bids, and Southern Railway submitted the high base bid of $995,000 per year. The Louisville & Nashville offered to lease the line for a base of $900,000 per year and followed up with an alternate bid that tied the lease to the railroad's earnings.

The State Properties Control Commission awarded the bid to Southern, but the General Assembly responded by asking the commission to revisit the lease. The Louisville & Nashville came out on top following the second round of bids with an offer that guaranteed the state at least $32.5 million over 25 years.

In 1967, in the midst of the lease fight, some lawmakers sought to sell the Western & Atlantic. "I don't believe in the state getting in business, but we have that railroad and I want to keep it," the *Atlanta Constitution* quoted Lt. Gov. George T. Smith as saying. The state did not sell the Western & Atlantic, and Gov. Lester Maddox signed the extension on March 4, 1968.

As the Louisville & Nashville extended its hold on the line, its focus was shifting away from passenger trains to freight. Its passenger train timetables of the era included advertisements for its freight services to attract new customers. In November 1965, the railroad announced the addition of a second *Dixie Piggyback Flyer* freight train running between Chicago and Jacksonville, Florida. The train made the run in a fast 36 hours.

The beginning of the end of passenger service came by July 1969 when the Louisville & Nashville asked the Interstate Commerce Commission to drop its passenger train between St. Louis and Atlanta. However, in December 1969, the federal board ordered the railroad to continue its twice-a-day-passenger service between the two cities.

In April 1971, the Louisville & Nashville said it planned to drop three of its four remaining passenger trains, including the *Georgian* running between St. Louis and Atlanta via Nashville. The train went out of service at the end of April, just before Amtrak took over many passenger operations nationwide.

Even after shedding its passenger train operations, the 1970s era was a difficult one for the Western & Atlantic. By 1978, the Louisville & Nashville issued several orders slowing how fast trains could operate over the line. Derailments were not uncommon, and a railroad consultant in May 1978 issued a report that declared the tracks to be unsafe. The Louisville & Nashville responded by repairing most of the deficient tracks along the line between Tilford Yard in northwest Atlanta and Chattanooga. The following year, federal regulators called the Louisville & Nashville one of the most accident-prone lines.

Despite the criticisms, the Louisville & Nashville continued to operate until December 1982, when it was formally merged into the Seaboard System Railroad. Although the railroad only existed for a short period, Seaboard System officials took the opportunity to extend their hold on the Western & Atlantic. As part of their pitch, railroad personnel took two dozen Georgia lawmakers and officials, including then lieutenant governor Zell Miller and state auditor G.W. Hogan, on a trip to Chattanooga.

In January 1986, the Georgia General Assembly approved a new 25-year lease once the current lease expired in 1994. The amended lease expires on December 31, 2019. Even though Southern officials bid for the Western & Atlantic two decades earlier, the railroad's successor, Norfolk Southern, declined to bid this time. The lease extension was overwhelmingly approved, but it came after some South Georgia lawmakers wanted to scuttle the deal to protest Seaboard's decision to eliminate freight service to some communities.

The *Atlanta Constitution* in November 1985 quoted a Seaboard vice president as saying, "the railroad is interested in the long term. This lease would provide that."

Even if railroad officials were thinking long term, their railroad was not long for the world. By 1986, the Seaboard System was part of CSX Transportation, the railroad that still leases the Western & Atlantic.

Photographer David W. Salter took this picture of Louisville & Nashville No. 756 pulling the *Georgian* north of Bolton on November 24, 1946. This was one of the first runs of the new train, which began service just a week earlier. (Courtesy of the Southern Museum of Civil War & Locomotive History Archives, David Salter Collection.)

Photographer George B. Mock Jr. captured Louisville & Nashville No. 760 as it pulled out of Atlanta's Union Station on August, 16, 1947. The EMD E7 engine was cobranded for both the Louisville & Nashville and Nashville, Chattanooga & St. Louis. (Courtesy of the Southern Museum of Civil War & Locomotive History Archives, David Salter Collection.)

The seven-car *Freedom Train*, above, traveled across the country from September 1947 until January 1949 and featured an exhibit of priceless historical documents, many from the National Archives. Below, Chattanooga mayor Hugh Wasson and Hamilton County judge Wilkes Thrasher headed a welcoming committee for the *Freedom Train*. The train visited Chattanooga's Union Depot in January 1948 following a two-day stay in Atlanta. After leaving Chattanooga, the train traveled to Nashville. (Above, courtesy of the National Archives; below, courtesy of the Chattanooga Public Library.)

A Chicago & Eastern Illinois locomotive pulls the *Georgian*, less than two years after it launched, as it approaches Atlanta's Jefferson Street at 7:45 a.m. on August 26, 1948. The Louisville & Nashville and the Nashville, Chattanooga & St. Louis partnered with the Chicago & Eastern Illinois to run the *Georgian* to Chicago. (Courtesy of the Southern Museum of Civil War & Locomotive History Archives, David Salter Collection.)

Photographer Shelby F. Lowe took this photograph of Nashville, Chattanooga & St. Louis train No. 5 running near Cartersville in 1954. That same year, following more than a year of negotiations, the Nashville, Chattanooga & St. Louis announced plans for a new rail yard in northwest Atlanta. (Courtesy of the Southern Museum of Civil War & Locomotive History Archives, David Salter Collection.)

Above, the *Georgian* waits to depart Atlanta's Union Station in October 1955. Below, the *Georgian* runs north of Bolton. In opening its new Hills Park Yard in October 1957, the Louisville & Nashville incorporated and modernized an existing Nashville, Chattanooga & St. Louis yard with the same name. In 1959, the railroad said it would rename the yard in honor of retiring president John E. Tilford. (Above, photograph by J. Parker Lamb, courtesy of the Center for Railroad Photography and Art; below, courtesy of the Southern Museum of Civil War & Locomotive History Archives, David Salter Collection.)

Much like its counterpart in Atlanta, the Louisville & Nashville used Chattanooga's Union Depot, pictured here around 1955, until 1971. The following year, the state put some of the property it owned in Chattanooga on the market, a development Chattanooga officials greeted with excitement. Georgia's ownership of some prime real estate in Chattanooga at times caused consternation and prompted city officials to threaten to condemn the land. "It hasn't been utilized properly. It has been like a cancer right in the heart of Chattanooga," the State Properties Commission director said in 1972. (Both, courtesy of the Chattanooga Public Library.)

Louisville & Nashville No. 781 pulls the *Georgian* through Vinings on November 28, 1956. Even though it was a relatively small community, Vinings remained a signal stop for the railroad until at least 1958. (Courtesy of the Southern Museum of Civil War & Locomotive History Archives, David Salter Collection.)

By the 1950s, passenger travel was beginning to wane, and many railroads, including the Louisville & Nashville, were nearing their final years of passenger operations. Still, that did not stop the railroad from promoting its service, as this advertisement from the Louisville & Nashville's fall 1958 timetable shows. One of the railroad's top trains was the *Georgian*, running between Chicago and Atlanta. (Courtesy of Railfanning.org.)

In advance of the centennial of the Great Locomotive Chase in April 1962, the Louisville & Nashville removed the *General* locomotive from Chattanooga and took it to Louisville for an overhaul that included the addition of modern air brakes and converting the steamer to burn oil. Its removal sparked a years-long legal battle that ended with the locomotive permanently residing in Kennesaw. (Courtesy of the Chattanooga Public Library.)

In April 1962, the *General* retraced the route of the Great Locomotive Chase along the historic Western & Atlantic, making stops in cities along the line, including Cartersville, where this photograph was taken. (Courtesy of the Bartow History Museum.)

In addition to retracing its April 12, 1862, run, the Louisville & Nashville sent the *General* locomotive on a national tour during the 1960s. It appeared at the 1964 New York World's Fair in Flushing, New York. Workers removed the *General*'s smokestack so it could safely pass beneath bridges during transport via water in the New York Harbor. The *General* last ran under her own steam in 1966. (Both, courtesy of the Adairsville Depot History Museum and Welcome Center.)

The Louisville & Nashville produced this booklet that was part history and part marketing collateral, as it both recounted the story of the Great Locomotive Chase and promoted the railroad's service: "Modern L. & N. passenger and freight trains now provide prompt, safe, courteous and reliable service to the nation's travelers and shippers to points all over the nation." (Courtesy of Railfanning.org.)

THE GREAT
LOCOMOTIVE CHASE
On The Western & Atlantic Railroad
APRIL 12, 1862

The thrilling Civil War story of the General, now America's Favorite Locomotive

Compliments of
LOUISVILLE & NASHVILLE RAILROAD
Louisville, Ky.

The Louisville & Nashville later ran the *Georgian* to Chicago in conjunction with the Chicago & Eastern Illinois Railroad. Here, workers clean the *Georgian*'s coaches at Union Station in Atlanta on April 15, 1963. (Photograph by Roger Puta.)

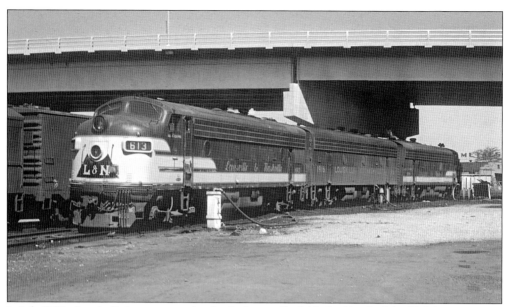

In July 1969, after declining passenger levels, the Louisville & Nashville asked the ICC for permission to discontinue the *Georgian*, which at the time operated between Atlanta and Evansville, Indiana. Here, Louisville & Nashville No. 631, an FP7, idles on a storage track at Union Station in Atlanta on April 15, 1963. (Photograph by Roger Puta.)

The *Georgian* waits to depart Union Station in Atlanta on November 25, 1967. By the latter half of the decade, the Louisville & Nashville operated only one passenger train over the Western & Atlantic, which arrived in Atlanta at 9:50 a.m. and departed at 5:15 p.m. "Otherwise the station is lifeless," the *Atlanta Constitution* wrote on December 23, 1969, of Union Station. It, too, was approaching the end of its life. (Photograph by Roger Puta.)

In 1969, the ICC criticized the Louisville & Nashville's service and ordered it to continue operating passenger trains between Atlanta and St. Louis. The railroad said it lost $688,000 on the service during the previous year. (Photograph by Roger Puta.)

In 1970, when this photograph was taken, the ICC held a series of hearings in Atlanta; Hopkinsville, Kentucky; Nashville, Tennessee; and St. Louis, Missouri, to determine whether to allow the Louisville & Nashville to discontinue the *Georgian*. At the Atlanta hearing in August 1970, six riders petitioned the ICC to prohibit the Louisville & Nashville from eliminating the train. Service ended in April 1971. (Photograph by Roger Puta.)

ST. LOUIS and EVANSVILLE

| READ DOWN | | Table D | READ UP |
No. 5 Daily	Miles	(Coaches Only) March 16, 1970	No. 10 Daily
4.30 PM	0	Lv St. Louis, Mo...............CST Ar	8.55 AM
4.48 PM	3	Lv East St. Louis, Ill.▲..........CST Ar	8.17 AM
5.20 PM	17	Lv Belleville ▲...............CST Lv	7.41 AM
6.05 PM	52	Lv Nashville, Ill.▲............CST Lv	f 6.58 AM
6.25 PM	63	Lv Ashley ▲..................CST Lv	3 6.44 AM
6.50 PM	79	Lv Mt. Vernon. Ill.▲..........CST Lv	6.19 AM
f 7.15 PM	94	Lv Dahlgren ▲................CST Lv	
7.30 PM	104	Lv McLeansboro ▲...........CST Lv	5.40 AM
A 7.47 PM	117	Lv Enfield ▲.................CST Lv	f 5.17 AM
8.05 PM	127	Lv Carmi▲Little Wabash River...CST Lv	5.04 AM
....E....	134	Lv Maunie, Ill.▲Wabash River...CST Lv	
8.35 PM	146	Lv Mt. Vernon, Ind.▲..........CST Lv	4.34 AM
9.30 PM	165	Ar Evansville, Ind............CST Lv	3.55 AM

EVANSVILLE and ATLANTA

| READ DOWN | | Table E | READ UP |
No. 3 Daily	Miles	(Coaches Only) March 16, 1970	No. 4 Daily
		Ohio River	
9.40 PM	0	Lv Evansville, Ind............CST Ar	3.40 AM
G10.02 PM	13	Lv Henderson, Ky.▲..........CST Lv	H 3.02 AM
H10.44 PM	52	Lv Madisonville ▲...........CST Lv	H 2.13 AM
H11.33 PM	87	Lv Hopkinsville ▲...........CST Lv	H 1.16 AM
....	111	Lv Guthrie, Ky. ▲............CST Lv	H12.42 AM
1.40 AM	159	Ar Nashville, Tenn...........CST Lv	11.45 PM
		Cumberland River	
2.00 AM	159	Lv Nashville, Tenn...........CST Ar	11.20 PM
3.24 AM	228	Lv Tullahoma ▲..............CST Lv	9.44 PM
6.30 AM	310	Ar Chattanooga, Tenn.........EST Lv	8.45 PM
		Tennessee River	
6.40 AM	310	Lv Chattanooga, Tenn.........EST Ar	8.30 PM
B 7.35 AM	348	Lv Dalton ▲.................EST Lv	B 7.23 PM
D 8.36 AM	399	Lv Cartersville▲Etowah River...EST Lv	D 6.25 PM
B 9.15 AM	424	Lv Marietta ▲...............EST Lv	B 5.51 PM
10.00 AM	444	Ar Atlanta, Ga...............EST Lv	5.15 PM

By April 1970, the Louisville & Nashville operated a single train running between Atlanta and Evansville, Indiana, over the Western & Atlantic, as the timetable at left shows. Atlanta's role as a railroad hub, at least from a passenger train standpoint, was severely diminished by October 1969, as the Atlanta Terminal Company's schedule below illustrates. The Georgia Railroad no longer used one of Atlanta's passenger depots, opting to use its freight depot for passenger service. The Louisville & Nashville was Union Station's sole tenant. (Both, courtesy of Railfanning.org.)

ATLANTA TERMINAL COMPANY

TERMINAL STATION
ATLANTA, GA.

TIME TABLE No. 19

IN EFFECT 12:01 A.M.   OCTOBER 27, 1969

EASTERN STANDARD TIME

FOR THE GOVERNMENT OF EMPLOYEES ONLY

SUBJECT TO CHANGE WITHOUT NOTICE

R. K. FINNELL
MANAGER

TERMINAL STATION
ARRIVING TRAINS

SOU	21	4:00 A.M.	Wash. Mail only
SOU	37	9:15 A.M.	New York
SOU	47	9:15 A.M.	New York
C of Ga	19	10:45 A.M.	Columbus
A&WP	38	11:15 A.M.	New Orleans
C of Ga	107	1:00 P.M.	Savannah
SOU	29	4:05 P.M.	Washington
SOU	48	6:40 P.M.	New Orleans
SOU	3	9:35 P.M.	Cincinnati

DEPARTING TRAINS

SOU	4	8:10 A.M.	Cincinnati
SOU	47	9:40 A.M.	New Orleans
SOU	38	11:35 A.M.	New York
C of Ga	108	6:00 P.M.	Savannah
C of Ga	20	6:15 P.M.	Columbus
SOU	48	7:00 P.M.	New York
A&WP	37	7:15 P.M.	New Orleans

UNION STATION

		ARRIVE	FROM
L & N	No. 3	10:55 A.M.	ST. LOUIS
		DEPART	FOR
L & N	No. 4	5:15 P.M.	ST. LOUIS

4 HUNTER ST., S. E.

		ARRIVE	FROM
GA RR	No. 1	11:00 A.M.	AUGUSTA
		DEPART	FOR
GA RR	No. 2	6:00 P.M.	AUGUSTA

Workers began tearing down Atlanta's Union Station in August 1971. The *Atlanta Constitution* quoted one worker on the demolition team as saying, "I really hate to see buildings like this go." A parking lot replaced the station. (Courtesy of the Southern Museum of Civil War & Locomotive History Archives, James Bogle Collection.)

The Louisville & Nashville operated until 1982. On December 29, 1982, the Seaboard Coast Line and Louisville & Nashville were merged into the Seaboard System Railroad. The railroad company was short-lived and became part of CSX on July 1, 1986. Here, trains wearing a "Family Lines" paint scheme operate in Atlanta in 1987. (Photograph by Roger Puta.)

CSX Transportation subsumed the Seaboard System Railroad on July 1, 1986, and with it the lease of the Western & Atlantic Railroad. Here, CSX No. 7525 is seen at Wauhatchie, Tennessee, on October 20, 1990. (Photograph by Barry R. Byington, courtesy of Railfanning.org.)

Six

THE MODERN ROAD

Following a spate of railroad consolidations during the 1970s and 1980s, a new railroad established in 1980 assumed the lease of the Western & Atlantic. CSX was created by merging railroads, including the Seaboard System Railroad in 1986. Because the Seaboard System negotiated an extension of the Western & Atlantic lease, CSX had control of the line until 2019.

The modern era of the Western & Atlantic is unlike any other in the history of the line. Because of the consolidations, today there are only a handful of large Class I railroads (defined as any railroad with operating revenues of at least $447.6 million annually) in the United States.

The Western & Atlantic is now a small part of CSX's network of 21,000 rail miles in 23 states, the District of Columbia, and two Canadian provinces. The Jacksonville, Florida–based railroad reported $11.4 billion in revenues in 2017. As of the end of 2015, CSX's national railroad network included 2,700 miles in Georgia. The railroad's system included the former routes of one-time competitors, including the Georgia Railroad's line between Atlanta and Augusta.

As the historic Western & Atlantic merged into CSX, its name in many ways began to fade. However, the Western & Atlantic was an integral part of the CSX network, and CSX officials undertook many initiatives to upgrade and modernize the line.

In 1993, the company rebuilt portions of the line, replacing aging wooden crossties with concrete crossties along a 23.5-mile stretch. In 1995, the railroad announced it would add a second track to a six-mile section of the line from Smyrna to just north of Marietta. Portions of the line were double-tracked until at least the late 1960s, but the railroad removed the second track when it ended passenger trains and local freight service in the area. However, the addition of the second track caused controversy when the railroad closed pedestrian crossings in Marietta. The city unsuccessfully sued the railroad in a bid to reopen the shuttered crossings.

"We need more track to run the tonnage we got," the *Atlanta Constitution* quoted a railroad official as saying in 1995. "Now we have delays."

One on-again, off-again issue that bubbled to the surface during this era was the possibility of running commuter trains along the Western & Atlantic. In 1993, Marietta mayor Joe Mack Wilson publicly discussed the idea of building a commuter station in the city's downtown, according to an article in the *Atlanta Constitution*. "What other right-of-way can you buy from here to Atlanta?" the newspaper quoted the mayor as saying the following year.

In 2000, state transportation board members mulled over asking the state to earmark revenues from the Western & Atlantic lease—roughly $6 million per year at the time—to help fund commuter rail. But, over the years, CSX has shown little interest in sharing its busy Atlanta-to-Chattanooga line with commuter trains.

"CSX is in the business of moving freight," the *Atlanta Journal-Constitution* quoted a CSX vice president as saying in 2011. "We don't want to do anything that will prevent our ability to move freight both today and in the future."

The commuter train discussion notwithstanding, CSX, much like its predecessors, helped commemorate the Great Locomotive Chase. In the early morning hours of April 12, 2012, community and railroad dignitaries gathered for an observance of the anniversary. Mark Mathews, the mayor of Kennesaw at the time, told a group gathered outside the city's historic depot that the Great Locomotive Chase was "a piece of our history that we remember, we memorialize and we honor."

In March 2017, the Cobb County Commission approved a resolution asking the state to maintain control of the line so passenger trains could one day operate along the corridor. The idea of running commuter trains on the line played a minor role in lease extension discussions. In 2017, state legislators also approved a measure allowing the State Properties Commission the authority to negotiate an extension of the lease.

That same month, CSX named longtime railroad executive E. Hunter Harrison as its new chief executive officer. "I know of no reason that this railroad can not become the greatest railroad in North America," Trains.com News Wire quoted Harrison as saying in April 2017. "You look at the hand you're dealt and you say look, what is the best way to operate and run this franchise."

Among the changes, CSX announced a plan to close Tilford Yard in Atlanta, where the company operated several rail facilities. The Louisville & Nashville opened the yard in 1957, incorporating much of the Nashville, Chattanooga & St. Louis's Hills Park Yard. Interestingly, in 1969, the State Properties Commission decided against the state purchase of Tilford Yard, according to a news account from the time.

In 2018, the State of Georgia and CSX agreed to a 50-year lease extension of the Western & Atlantic Railroad, giving CSX control of the line until 11:59 p.m. on December 31, 2069. As part of the agreement, CSX agreed to sell 2.3 miles of unused rail corridor to the state for $10. The state plans to use the land to extend the Silver Comet Trail, a rails-to-trails path built on the former Seaboard Air Line Railroad between Atlanta and Birmingham, Alabama.

CSX is expected to pay the State of Georgia at least $1.2 billion over the next 50 years under the lease. Many transit proponents heralded a provision leaving open the door for commuter rail to run along the corridor, but as of 2019, only freight trains operate over the historic line. The Western & Atlantic started as a state-operated railroad, then became a leased railroad, and finally leased property comprised of approximately 1,550 acres over a distance of 173.33 miles between Atlanta and Chattanooga.

After assuming the Western & Atlantic lease, CSX continued maintenance and modernization of the historic line. In 1993, the company undertook a major overhaul of the line, replacing wooden crossties with concrete ties on a 23.5-mile stretch between the Chattahoochee River and Kennesaw, where this track maintenance equipment was photographed on a side track in the early 2000s. (Both photographs by Todd DeFeo; courtesy of Railfanning.org.)

By the late 1980s, CSX was one of two Class I railroads operating in Georgia. Above, a southbound CSX freight train passes through Moon's Station. The community was a wood shed and water tank where trains stopped to replenish their locomotives' fuel supply. Today, it is part of Kennesaw. Below, a CSX freight train rumbles through Kennesaw in May 2013. (Both photographs by Todd DeFeo; courtesy of Railfanning.org.)

In honor of the sesquicentennial of the Great Locomotive Chase in April 2012, CSX sent an executive train to join in the festivities in Kennesaw, Georgia. The F40PH-2 at the lead of the train was historic in its own right, dating to 1978. The locomotive served Amtrak and the Ohio Central before CSX purchased it. (Photograph by Todd DeFeo; courtesy of Railfanning.org.)

CSX maintained several sidings where it could park its track maintenance equipment, including this one in downtown Kennesaw as seen in August 2012. The railroad, which upgraded the siding in advance of the sesquicentennial in April 2012, later removed the side track. (Photograph by Todd DeFeo, courtesy of Railfanning.org.)

The population of Atlanta and its surrounding suburbs increased substantially in recent decades, at times causing conflicts between the public and the railroad. During the 1990s, the railroad closed several grade crossings in Marietta, prompting the city to sue. In 1998, lawmakers in the state house passed a resolution urging CSX to reopen a pair of pedestrian crossings in use since 1978. (Photograph by Todd DeFeo, courtesy of Railfanning.org.)

A southbound CSX freight passes through a double-tracked section of the Western & Atlantic. Leaders of the city took their bid to reopen the closed railroad crossings to the Georgia Supreme Court. The state's highest court in 2000 ruled against the city, and the crossings in question remained closed. (Photograph by Todd DeFeo, courtesy of Railfanning.org.)

Cartersville remains an important junction for CSX. The railroad's Junta Yard is located just north of town, and its line to Knoxville, Tennessee, splits from the Western & Atlantic. Here, a northbound freight passes the historic Cartersville depot in 2018. (Photograph by Todd DeFeo, courtesy of Railfanning.org.)

In another sign of the changing relationship between the railroad and nearby communities, in 2010 city officials in Smyrna, where this photograph was taken in August 2011, approved quiet zones at grade crossings near the town's downtown. With the new zones, trains are no longer required to sound horns at these crossings. (Photograph by Todd DeFeo, courtesy of Railfanning.org.)

Some communities along the Western & Atlantic, including Dalton, where this picture was taken in July 2017, have embraced the Western & Atlantic and its history, marketing itself as a popular place for watching trains. At Dalton, two rail lines cross in the heart of the city, and dozens of trains pass through town every day. Similarly in Ringgold, officials built a train-viewing platform directly across from the 1850 train station, where these pictures were taken. (Both photographs by Todd DeFeo, courtesy of Railfanning.org.)

Coal is one of the many commodities CSX transports over the Western & Atlantic today. In 2017, coal represented 18 percent of CSX's revenue and 13 percent of its volume. Above, a southbound CSX coal train idles next to the Southern Museum of Civil War & Locomotive History in downtown Kennesaw in July 2017. Below, a pusher locomotive helps a southbound coal train in Smyrna in January 2017. (Both photographs by Todd DeFeo, courtesy of Railfanning.org.)

Unlike in previous eras, the Western & Atlantic line today is well-maintained. CSX spent more than $765 million for maintenance-of-way efforts system wide in 2017. Progressive Railroading quoted the company in April 2017 as saying, "CSX continuously reviews its investments in maintenance and infrastructure upgrades to ensure the railroad continues to deliver safe, reliable service for customers." Here, a work truck passes by the historic Tunnel Hill depot in 2018. (Photograph by Todd DeFeo, courtesy of Railfanning.org.)

In September 2018, the Georgia State Properties Commission and CSX signed a new 50-year lease for the Western & Atlantic line. The new agreement could bring in $1.2 billion in revenues to the state during its term, according to newspaper reports about the new deal. (Photograph by Todd DeFeo, courtesy of Railfanning.org.)

Seven

PRESERVING THE WESTERN & ATLANTIC

The final chapter of the life of the Western & Atlantic is unfinished, since preserving the railroad remains an ongoing task. In his October 1, 1862, report, Western & Atlantic superintendent John S. Rowland expressed his opinion that the railroad would stand as a monument to those who helped make it a reality.

"During the short time I have been connected with this Road, I am more firmly fixed in the opinion, which I have long entertained, that it is the greatest State investment in this Government, and that, under proper management, it becomes an inestimable blessing to every citizen of our great State, and that will be a lasting monument to the wise and good men who originated the great work," Rowland noted.

Today, much of the public may not realize the State of Georgia still owns the route. Communities up and down the line have staked their claims to a portion of its history and that of the Great Locomotive Chase, and today, there are at least a half-dozen museums along the Western & Atlantic that tell at least a small portion of the line's story.

The Western & Atlantic used hundreds of locomotives throughout its history. However, only two—the *General* and *Texas*—survive.

Perhaps more important than the physical upgrades the Nashville, Chattanooga & St. Louis made to the Western & Atlantic when it leased the line was the railroad's many tributes to the route's history, notably the Great Locomotive Chase of 1862.

When the Nashville, Chattanooga & St. Louis leased the line starting in 1890, the railroad took possession of the *General*. In many ways, the famed steamer assumed the role as the public face of the Western & Atlantic. In 1901, for example, the railroad placed monuments in Kennesaw and Ringgold, marking the beginning and end of the Great Locomotive Chase. That same year, the railroad put the *General* on display in Chattanooga's Union Station.

Years later, when the Louisville & Nashville removed the *General* from Union Depot in Chattanooga under cover of darkness, it set off a multiyear dispute about who owned the locomotive and how to preserve it. The railroad refurbished the steam engine for the centennial of the Great Locomotive Chase.

In 1967, the Louisville & Nashville planned to move the *General* from Louisville to Kennesaw via Chattanooga. When the train arrived in Chattanooga, Mayor Ralph Kelley and a group of deputies obstructed the tracks, forcing the train to stop. The City of Chattanooga sued the Louisville & Nashville. The railroad ultimately prevailed after the US Supreme Court declined to hear the case. That paved the way for the Louisville & Nashville to donate the locomotive to the State of Georgia.

In February 1972, Louisville & Nashville president W.H. Kendall officially gave the locomotive to the State of Georgia, when he presented the deed to Gov. Jimmy Carter.

At the same time, the railroad also preserved the *Texas*. In 1908, the Nashville, Chattanooga & St. Louis donated the locomotive to the City of Atlanta, which placed it on display in Atlanta's Grant Park. In 1927, the city moved the *Texas* to the basement of the Cyclorama building, which was also home to an 1886 painting depicting the Battle of Atlanta.

"Atlanta is the place for the keeping of this engine," Wilbur G. Kurtz said in 1911 of the *Texas*, according to the Atlanta History Center. "The participants in the pursuit of Andrews lived here: the subsequent history of the raiders is indissolubly connected with the town, and Atlanta herself, from the time she left off being Marthasville, owes her present prosperity to the railroads."

In 1936, Kurtz oversaw several upgrades to the locomotive, including a pilot (or cowcatcher), a new smokestack, and nameplates. He also painted the *Texas* so it would resemble its 1862 appearance. In 2014, the City of Atlanta and the Atlanta History Center signed a 75-year agreement to transfer the Battle of Atlanta painting and the *Texas* to a to-be-built facility at the Atlanta History Center. Before moving the locomotive to the museum, officials sent it to the North Carolina Transportation Museum in Spencer, North Carolina. There, Steam Operations Corporation restored the *Texas* to its 1880s appearance.

The *Texas* returned to its new home at the Atlanta History Center in 2017. In November 2018, the Atlanta History Center opened a new exhibit, Texas, Locomotion: Railroads and the Making of Atlanta, with the steamer at the center.

"As railroads are Atlanta's reason for being, this steam engine is an icon of Atlanta's founding and growth as the Gate City of the South—the commercial center of the Southeast," Atlanta History Center president and CEO Sheffield Hale said. "The Texas locomotive symbolizes Atlanta's longtime relationship with railroads and the city's importance as a hub for people, commerce, and ideas. No artifact can be more important for telling the story of Atlanta's beginnings than this Western & Atlantic locomotive."

Bodwell E. Wells, the Western & Atlantic's civil engineer, began placing more permanent stone mileposts in the fall of 1850, including Zero Milepost in Atlanta. A city charter approved on February 28, 1874, established Atlanta's city limits as a circle a mile and half in every direction from Zero Milepost. In 2018, Zero Milepost was moved to the Atlanta History Center. (Courtesy of the Southern Museum of Civil War & Locomotive History Archives, James Bogle Collection.)

Ohio's tribute to the Andrews Raiders was unveiled on May 30, 1891, at the Chattanooga National Cemetery. Surviving raiders traveled from California, Iowa, Kansas, Ohio, Oklahoma, and Nebraska for the unveiling. Raider William Pittenger later wrote it was "a perfect and sabbath-like day." (Courtesy of the Library of Congress Prints and Photographs Division.)

The *General* retired from active service in 1891 and was later stored on a siding in Vinings. Photographer E. Warren Clark located the engine and asked Nashville, Chattanooga & St. Louis president John W. Thomas to restore the *General* for exhibition at the World's Columbian Exposition in Chicago (the Chicago World's Fair) in 1893. (Courtesy of the Southeastern Railway Museum.)

In 1901, the Nashville, Chattanooga & St. Louis placed monuments made from white Georgia marble in Kennesaw and Ringgold, marking the beginning and the end of the Great Locomotive Chase. A tablet mounted on the monuments offers a brief retelling of the chase and the names of the men who participated in the daring event. (Both photographs by Todd DeFeo, courtesy of Railfanning.org.)

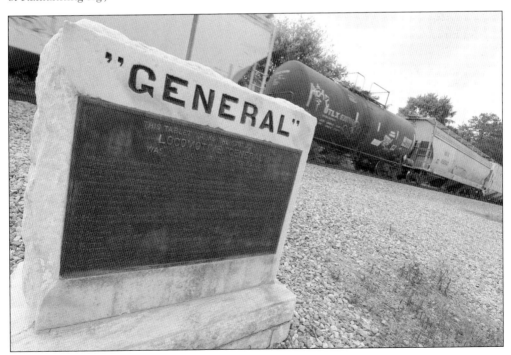

In 1901, the Nashville, Chattanooga & St. Louis sent the *General* to Chattanooga. There, it was placed on "permanent" display in Chattanooga's Union Depot, as shown in this picture from 1907. (Courtesy of the Library of Congress.)

THE "GENERAL" USED BY ANDREW'S RAIDERS, NOW ON EXHIBITION, UNION DEPOT, CHATTANOOGA, TENN.

In 1926, the *General* steamed up for use in a motion picture and reportedly reached speeds of 55 miles per hour. The *General* left Chattanooga's Union Depot to travel to high-profile events, including the Baltimore & Ohio Railroad's Fair of the Iron Horse in 1927, the Century of Progress Exhibition in Chicago in 1933, the New York World's Fair in 1939, and the Chicago Railroad Fair in 1948. (Courtesy of Railfanning.org.)

This 1903 picture of the *Texas* operating in Emerson may be the last photograph of the locomotive in operation; it was removed from service in 1907. William Mason & Company in Taunton, Massachusetts, likely built the *Texas's* current tender in 1864 for the US Military Railroad locomotive *Dalton*. The Western & Atlantic purchased the *Dalton* and renamed it for William McRae, the railroad's general superintendent and a former Confederate brigadier general. (Courtesy of the Atlanta History Center.)

Anthony Murphy, a native of Ireland, was the Western & Atlantic's repair shop foreman in 1862. He joined William Fuller in pursuing the *General* during the 1862 Great Locomotive Chase. Here, he poses next to the *Texas* in 1907, when the locomotive was numbered 212 and carried the markings of the Nashville, Chattanooga & St. Louis. (Courtesy of the Atlanta History Center.)

The *Atlanta Georgian and News* on the front page of its August 2, 1907, edition highlighted the famed *Texas's* poor condition. The newspaper launched a campaign to save the locomotive from the scrapyard. "Let every boy and girl in Georgia, who loves the state and glories in its traditions, contribute what he or she feels like and can afford," the newspaper requested. (Courtesy of the Digital Library of Georgia.)

In 1927, Atlanta moved the locomotive to the basement of the new Cyclorama, a massive 360-degree painting of the Battle of Atlanta. In an odd twist, workers moving the locomotive left it overnight on South Boulevard, and an Ohio motorist crashed into it while it was sitting in the street. "The automobile came off second best in the collision," the *Atlanta Constitution* noted. (Courtesy of Railfanning.org.)

115

The *Texas*, built in New Jersey by Danforth, Cooke & Co. in 1856, remained at the Cyclorama, pictured above in a 1930s- or 1940s-era postcard, in Atlanta until December 2015. In 2014, the Atlanta History Center and the City of Atlanta signed a 75-year license agreement to relocate the Battle of Atlanta Cyclorama and the *Texas*, pictured below in June 2011, to a new space at the Atlanta History Center. (Above, courtesy of the Tichnor Brothers Collection, Boston Public Library; below, photograph by Todd DeFeo, courtesy of Railfanning.org)

After its removal from the Cyclorama, the historic steam engine traveled to the North Carolina Transportation Museum in Spencer, North Carolina, for a 15-month restoration, which returned the locomotive to its 1880s appearance. Here, the newly refurbished *Texas* is unveiled to the public on the North Carolina museum's 1924 turntable on April 28, 2017. (Courtesy of the Atlanta History Center.)

The *Texas* returned to Atlanta in May 2017, when it was relocated to the Atlanta History Center. Here, the *Texas* is gently lowered onto original 1880s-era tracks at the Atlanta History Center by the Georgia Rigging Company. Once the locomotive was put in place, the museum erected a glass-walled exhibit area. (Courtesy of the Atlanta History Center.)

In 1972, the *General* moved into what was then known as the Big Shanty Museum, later renamed the Kennesaw Civil War Museum. Starting in 2001, the museum underwent a two-year renovation that enlarged the facility to nearly 50,000 square feet. It houses three permanent exhibits, including the *General*, pictured below in July 2017. The expanded museum continued to interpret the Great Locomotive Chase and also highlighted how the Western & Atlantic helped postwar Georgia recover. The museum is today a Smithsonian affiliate. (Above, courtesy of the Southern Museum of Civil War & Locomotive History Archives, James Bogle Collection; below, photograph by Todd DeFeo, courtesy of Railfanning.org.)

After the historic tunnel in Tunnel Hill, pictured above in 2018, was replaced by a larger opening in 1928, the old opening through Chetoogeta Mountain was abandoned and fell into a state of disrepair. In the 1990s, preservationists sought to save the aging structure, and in the mid-1990s, the State of Georgia transferred ownership of the tunnel to the City of Tunnel Hill. The tunnel reopened to the public in 2000 for its 150th anniversary. (Both photographs by Todd DeFeo, courtesy of Railfanning.org.)

The Tunnel Hill railroad depot, pictured in July 2017, was built using limestone from nearby Chetoogeta Mountain beginning in 1848. In 1861, Confederate president Jefferson Davis gave a speech at the depot, and Sherman later used the building as his headquarters. In 2013, Georgia Trust for Historic Preservation named the railroad depot and nine other structures in Georgia to its Places in Peril list. (Photograph by Todd DeFeo, courtesy of Railfanning.org.)

The Nashville, Chattanooga & St. Louis built the Marietta depot in 1898. The Louisville & Nashville daily train between Evansville and Atlanta continued to serve the depot into the 1970s. The depot, pictured here in August 2015, is today home to the Marietta Welcome Center. (Photograph by Todd DeFeo, courtesy of Railfanning.org.)

The Nashville, Chattanooga & St. Louis built the Kennesaw depot in 1908, and two passenger waiting rooms were added during the 1920s. In 1998, the City of Kennesaw restored the exterior of the structure. The depot, pictured here in July 2017, today houses a small museum focused on local history. (Photograph by Todd DeFeo, courtesy of Railfanning.org.)

Portions of the Cartersville depot, pictured in February 2012, date to 1854. The depot was heavily damaged during the Civil War, and the Nashville, Chattanooga & St. Louis remodeled the depot in 1902, with work completed by local contractor Eugene Smith. The Louisville & Nashville in 1972 demolished the southern portion of the historic structure. The remaining portion today houses the city's welcome center. (Photograph by Todd DeFeo, courtesy of Railfanning.org.)

The Nashville, Chattanooga & St. Louis built the Adairsville depot in 1891. The structure is home to the Adairsville Depot History Museum and Welcome Center, which reopened in 2017. Adairsville also hosts the annual Great Locomotive Chase Festival, a fall festival the city has held since 1968. (Photograph by Todd DeFeo, courtesy of Railfanning.org.)

Ringgold claims the oldest depot on the Western & Atlantic, with its structure dating to May 9, 1850, the day the full run of the Western & Atlantic began operations. As such, it is one of the few antebellum depots still standing in Georgia. The edifice, pictured here in June 2018, today is home to a special event space. (Photograph by Todd DeFeo, courtesy of Railfanning.org.)

Jacob Stroup established an ironworks in Emerson in the 1830s and later sold his business to politician Mark Anthony Cooper. In 1858–1859, Cooper built the Etowah Railroad, a roughly five-mile line that connected the ironworks with the Western & Atlantic. Cooper sold the ironworks to the Confederate States of America in 1863, and Union troops destroyed it the following year. This smokestack, pictured in April 2015, is all that remains of the ironworks. (Photograph by Todd DeFeo, courtesy of Railfanning.org.)

The bridge over the Etowah River near Emerson, completed around 1847, remained in service until the 1940s. After the Western & Atlantic was realigned, the piers of the bridge, one of which is pictured here in June 2018, remained standing in the middle of the river. (Photograph by Todd DeFeo, courtesy of Railfanning.org.)

The Western & Atlantic built the Dalton depot in 1852 as a combination passenger and freight depot. For many years, a restaurant occupied the historic building. However, by July 2018, when this picture was taken, the depot was abandoned, and the Georgia Trust for Historic Preservation and the City of Dalton teamed up to sell the structure to a buyer who would restore it. (Above, photograph by Todd DeFeo, courtesy of Railfanning.org; below, courtesy of the Georgia Trust for Historic Preservation.)

Even though the railroad bypassed Allatoona Pass 70 years ago, the former railroad bed is today a popular destination for hikers. In addition to the trail through the railroad pass, the site interprets the preserved remains of earthworks and trenches from the bloody Battle of Allatoona Pass. (Photograph by Todd DeFeo, courtesy of Railfanning.org.)

The Kennesaw House in Marietta is one of the city's oldest buildings and is a former cotton warehouse and hotel. Union spies spent the night here before boarding the morning train during the Great Locomotive Chase. Today, the building is home to the Marietta Museum of History, offering a series of exhibits dedicated to the city's history and the Great Locomotive Chase. (Photograph by Todd DeFeo, courtesy of Railfanning.org.)

BIBLIOGRAPHY

Caldwell, Wilber W. *The Courthouse and the Depot*. Macon, GA: Mercer University Press, 2001.

DeFeo, Todd. "Western & Atlantic Railroad." Railfanning.org/western-atlantic/. 2018.

Duncan, Russell. "Rufus Bullock (1834–1907)." www.georgiaencyclopedia.org/articles/government-politics/rufus-bullock-1834-1907. 2004.

Garrett, Franklin M. *Atlanta and Environs: A Chronicle of Its People and Events, 1820s–1870s: Volume 1*. Athens, GA: University of Georgia Press, 2011.

Herr, Kincaid. *Louisville & Nashville Railroad 1850–1963*. Louisville, KY: University Press of Kentucky, 1964.

Johnston, James Houstoun. *Western and Atlantic Railroad of the State of Georgia*. Atlanta, GA: Stein Printing Co., 1932.

Klein, Maury. *History of the Louisville & Nashville Railroad*. New York, NY: Macmillan Publishing Company, 1972.

Phillips, Ulrich Bonnell. "An American State-Owned Railroad." *Yale Review*. 259–282. 1906.

Pittinger, William. *Daring & Suffering*. Nashville, TN: Cumberland House Publishing, 1999.

Prince, Richard E. *Nashville, Chattanooga and St. Louis Railway: History and Steam Locomotives*. Bloomington, IN: Indiana University Press, 2001.

Range, Willard. "Hannibal I. Kimball." *The Georgia Historical Quarterly* Vol. 29, No. 2. (1945): 47–70.

Roth, Darlene R. and Andy Ambrose. *Metropolitan Frontiers*. Atlanta, GA: Longstreet Press, 1996.

Stover, John F. "Georgia Railroads During the Reconstruction Years." *Railroad History* No. 134. (1976): 56–65.

Strickland, Justin W. *Chattanooga's Terminal Station*. Charleston, SC: Arcadia Publishing, 2009.

Winn, Les R. *Ghost Trains & Depots of Georgia*. Chamblee, GA: Big Shanty Publishing Co., 1995.

DISCOVER THOUSANDS OF LOCAL HISTORY BOOKS FEATURING MILLIONS OF VINTAGE IMAGES

Arcadia Publishing, the leading local history publisher in the United States, is committed to making history accessible and meaningful through publishing books that celebrate and preserve the heritage of America's people and places.

Find more books like this at
www.arcadiapublishing.com

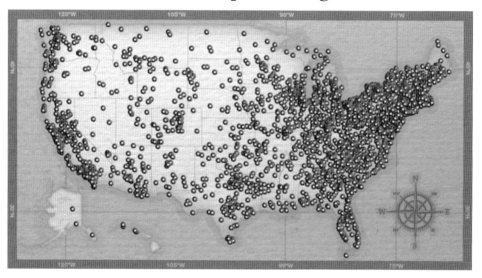

Search for your hometown history, your old stomping grounds, and even your favorite sports team.

Consistent with our mission to preserve history on a local level, this book was printed in South Carolina on American-made paper and manufactured entirely in the United States. Products carrying the accredited Forest Stewardship Council (FSC) label are printed on 100 percent FSC-certified paper.

MADE IN THE USA